INDIA & THE UNITED NATIONS

P. JAYACHANDRA RAJU

OrangeBooks Publication

Smriti Nagar, Bhilai, Chhattisgarh - 490020

Website: **www.orangebooks.in**

First Edition, 2022
ISBN: 978-93-92878-26-8

INDIA
AND THE
UNITED NATIONS

OrangeBooks Publication

www.orangebooks.in

Foreword

Almost at the end of World War II, the United Nations Organization was bom in October 1945 with the active participation, thought processes and ratification of its charter by the major players including China, France, the Soviet Union, the United States of America and the United Kingdom.

The Organization was formed primarily to safeguard social democracy, freedom and world peace. Since then, the founding countries continue to wield most power despite the evolving changes and imbalances in demographics, geographical environmental effects, rapid technological developments, human migrations and associated social norms.

Till date, the UN remains the largest, in fact only, international body to attend to international conflicts and internal conflicts that affect the neighboring countries issues that impact the global environment; human well-being and development; International trade, relations, and cooperation; education and sustainable development.

Among others, India despite being one of the largest troop contributing countries to the United Nations Peacekeeping Operations world-wide, poised to be the third largest economy in the world with a large cosmopolitan, multi-lingual, multireligious and multi-cultural population, is yet to be recognized for a permanent seat in United Nations.

It is lamentable that only a small segment of our population is aware of the role and functioning of international organizations akin to the United Nations in global peace, economics, political dynamics, international standards and recommended practices as laid down by specialized institutions and global environmental researchers, practitioners and advocates.

By nature, we can never be independent, we are interdependent. We are social beings and can never be in isolation. Knowledge and exposure promotes awareness of threats and opportunities, strengths and weaknesses. Planet Earth's resources are limited and unequally distributed. Every living being has its own role to play in sustenance and for harmonious coexistence, humans have an essential role to play in mutual understanding, cooperation, sharing, conservation and protection.

The author-compiler of this book, Mr Jayachandra Raju, is an aviation professional with internationally acclaimed experience, an academician, philanthropist, and an environmentalist; above all, he is a man deeply concerned about social welfare. He has been at the forefront of volunteering services for several just causes and actively lends his support and expertise to any activity or service for ocial development. He is an avid advocate of environment protection and a keen supporter of global sustainable development.

As part of the United Nations Organization, he has served in various countries around the world. He has served the Indian as well as the International Aviation industry in various capacities.

Mr Jayachandra Raju's services and competence are widely recognised as is evident in the number of awards he has been conferred upon for his social and professional services.

The book is the culmination of his intent and effort to provide a concise reference on the UN and India's role in it, to students, knowledge seekers and general readers.

He is indebted to all those who encouraged him to undertake this task and to those who supported him in vetting and shaping up his compilations to be as presentable as possible.The views expressed herein are those of the author(s) and do not necessarily reflect the views of the United Nations.

About the author

Jayachandra Raju, the author-compiler of this book, is an experienced aviation professional with a deep concern for societal well-being. He is an academician, philanthropist, and an environmentalist in equal measure and continues to render tireless service.

As part of the United Nations Organization, he has served in various countries across continents. He has served as Instructor and Advisor to civil aviation authorities of Somalia, Kenya, Former Yugoslavia, Democratic Republic of Congo, Republic of Nepal, Republic of Sudan in United Nations Missions.

He has served the Indian as well as the International Aviation sector in various capacities as Inspector, Air Traffic Controller, Aerodrome Officer, Flight Operations Officer, Project Manager and Quality Assurance Officer.

Raju has organized international seminars and conferences and presented the view points of the United Nations to "North Atlantic Treaty Organization" (NATO) of Europe, International Civil Aviation Organization (ICAO) – Canada and the International Air Transport Association (IATA) – Canada.

His penchant for service goes a long way back. As a young man, he organized medical/eye camps in rural and remote areas in India and readily volunteered for social service. He is an ardent advocate of environment protection and a staunch votary of global sustainable development.

A committed philanthropist and a thorough professional, many accolades and awards have followed Jayachandra Raju. Listed below are a significant few:

- The "Global Indian of the year 2013" for his distinctive services globally, by Hon. Pratibha Patil, the former President of India, in the National Integration Conference held in Pune in the year 2013.

- The "Dr. APJ Abdul Kalam Award" for the year 2018 in the "National Integration & Economic Growth Conference" held in New Delhi in the year 2018, for outstanding individual achievements and distinguished services to the Nation.

- The "Mahatma Gandhi Samman" for the year 2018, by the NRI Welfare Society of United Kingdom in the Conference held in House of Commons, London, for his contributions and achievements in keeping the Indian tricolour flying high.

- The Karnataka Suvarnashree Award, felicitated by the Maharaja of Mysore in Bangalore in 2019.

Through this book, he reaches out to learners - young and old. The book is the result of his effort to introduce the United Nations and its contribution to the world. It is envisaged to provide a concise reference for students, knowledge seekers and general readers alike.

TABLE OF CONTENTS

Chapter 1

-Section 1

-Section 2

-Section 3

Chapter 2

Chapter 3

Chapter 1

-Section 1

History in Brief
United Nations Charter: Preamble
Main Organs of the UN

-Section 2

India at the United Nations
UN Committees and India

-Section 3

UN Women
Women in the UN

-Section 1

History in Brief

The first half of the 20th Century was witness to two world wars that had left great parts of the world in ruins. Fifty nations from across the globe came together in quest of peace and progress and drafted the United Nations Charter in San Francisco, California from 25 April to 26 June 1945.

The UN officially came into existence on 24 October 1945 after the Charter was ratified by China, France, the then Soviet Union, the United Kingdom, the United States and most other signatories including India.

The main bodies of the UN are the General Assembly, the Security Council, the Economic and Social Council, the Trusteeship Council, the International Court of Justice, and the UN Secretariat. All the bodies were established.

United Nations Charter: Preamble

WE THE PEOPLES OF THE UNITED NATIONS DETERMINED

to save succeeding generations from the scourge of war, which twice in our lifetime has brought untold sorrow to mankind, and

to reaffirm faith in fundamental human rights, in the dignity and worth of the human person, in the equal rights of men and women and of nations large and small, and

to establish conditions under which justice and respect for the obligations arising from treaties and other sources of international law can be maintained, and

to promote social progress and better standards of life in larger freedom,

AND FOR THESE ENDS

to practice tolerance and live together in peace with one another as good neighbours, and

to unite our strength to maintain international peace and security, and to ensure, by the acceptance of principles and the institution of methods, that armed force shall not be used, save in the common interest, and

to employ international machinery for the promotion of the economic and social advancement of all peoples,

HAVE RESOLVED TO COMBINE OUR EFFORTS TO ACCOMPLISH THESE AIMS.

Accordingly, our respective Governments, through representatives assembled in the city of San Francisco, who have exhibited their full powers found to be in good and due form, have agreed to the present Charter of the United Nations and do hereby establish an international organization to be known as the United Nations.

Main Organs of the United Nations

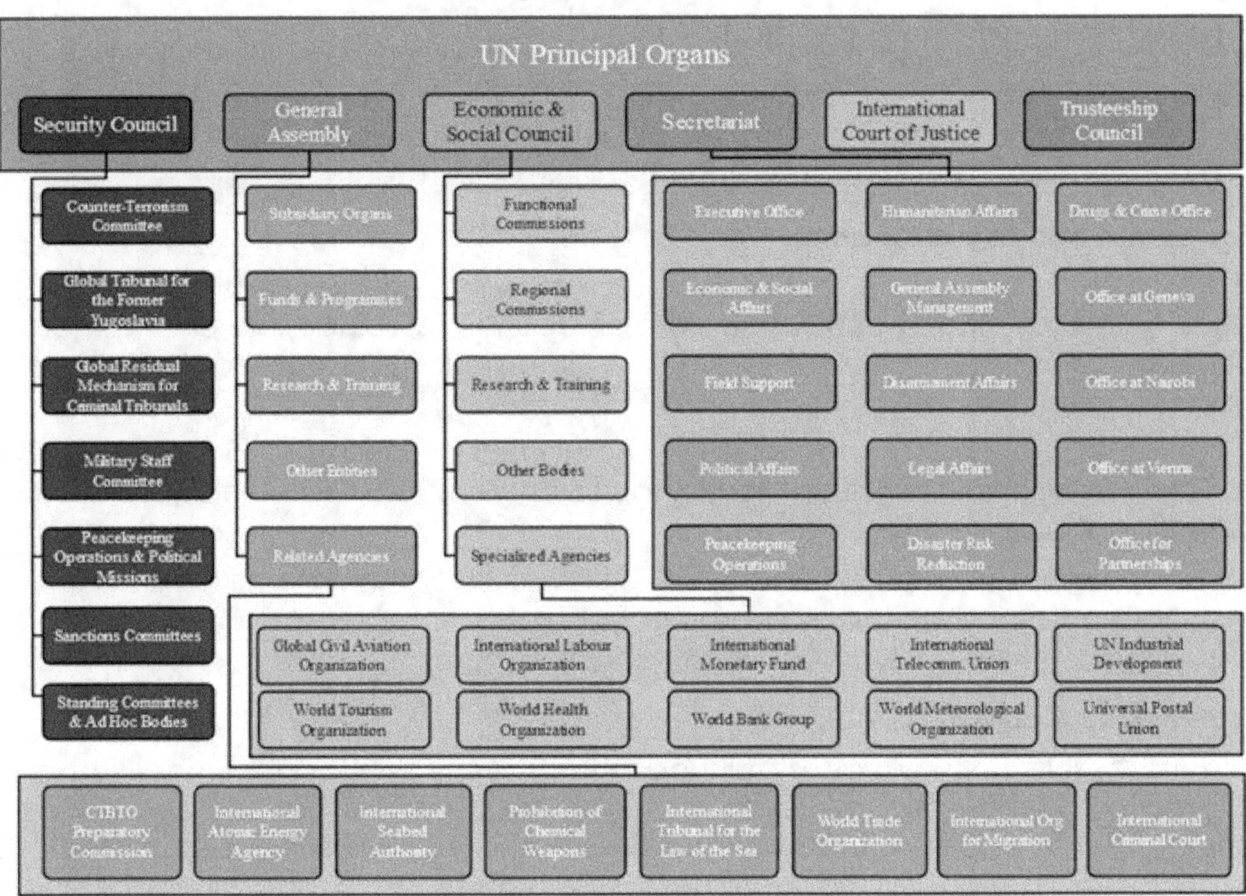

The main organs of the UN are the General Assembly, Security Council, Economic and Social Council, Trusteeship Council, International Court of Justice, and UN Secretariat. All were set up in 1945 when the UN was founded.

General Assembly

The General Assembly is the main deliberative, policymaking and representative organ of the UN. All 193 member states of the UN are represented in the General Assembly, making it the only UN body with universal   representation.

Each year, in September, the full UN membership meets in the General Assembly Hall in New York for the annual session, and general debate, where heads of state or their ambassadors attend and address.

Decisions on important questions, such as those on peace and security, admission of new members and budgetary matters, require a two-thirds majority vote of the General Assembly. Decisions on other questions are by simple majority. The General Assembly, each year, elects a GA President to serve a one-year term of office.

Security Council

The UN Security Council has the primary responsibility (under the UN Charter), to maintain international peace and security. It has 15 members (5 permanent and 10 non-permanent members). Each member has one vote. Under the Charter, all member states are obliged to comply with Council's decisions. The Security Council takes the lead in determining the threat perception to peace. It calls upon warring parties (or those involved in dispute) to settle it by peaceful means and facilitates methods of adjustment or terms of settlement. In some cases, the Security Council can resort to imposing sanctions or even authorize the use of force to maintain or restore international peace and security. The Security Council has a Presidency, which rotates, and changes, every month.

Economic and Social Council

The Economic and Social Council is the principal body for coordination, policy review, policy dialogue and suggestions on economic, social, and environmental issues. It also oversees the implementation of internationally agreed development goals.

It serves as the central mechanism for activities of the UN ecosphere and its specialized agencies in the economic, social, and environmental fields, supervising subsidiary and expert bodies.

It has 54 members, elected by the UN General Assembly for overlapping three-year terms. It is the United Nations' central platform for reflection, debate, and innovative thinking on sustainable development.

Trusteeship Council

The Trusteeship Council was established in 1945 by the UN Charter, under Chapter XIII, to provide international supervision for 11 Trust Territories that had been placed under the administration of seven member states, and ensure that adequate steps were taken to prepare the territories for self-government and independence. By 1994, all Trust Territories had attained self-government or independence. The Trusteeship Council suspended operation on November 1, 1994. By a resolution adopted on May 25, 1994, the Council amended its rules of procedure to drop the obligation to meet annually and agreed to meet as occasion required -- by its decision or the decision of its President, or at the request of a majority of its members or the General Assembly or the Security Council.

International Court of Justice

The International Court of Justice is the principal judicial organ of the United Nations. Its seat is at the Peace Palace in The Hague (Netherlands). It is the only one of the six principal organs of the United Nations not located in New York.

The Court's role is to settle, in accordance with international law, legal disputes submitted to it by states and to give advisory opinions on legal questions referred to it by authorized United Nations organs and specialized agencies.

Secretariat

The Secretariat comprises the Secretary-General and tens of thousands of international UN staff members who carry out the day-to-day work of the UN as mandated by the General Assembly and the Organization's other principal organs.

The Secretary-General is chief administrative officer of the organization, appointed by the General Assembly on the recommendation of the Security Council for a five-year, renewable term.

UN staff members are recruited internationally and locally, and work in duty stations and on peacekeeping missions all around the world. But serving the cause of peace in a violent world is a dangerous occupation. Since the founding of the United Nations, hundreds of brave men and women have given their lives in its service.

Functions and Powers of the General Assembly

According to the Charter of the United Nations, the General Assembly may:

- Consider and make recommendations on the general principles of cooperation for maintaining international peace and security, including disarmament
- Discuss any question relating to international peace and security and, except where a dispute or situation is currently being discussed by the Security Council, make recommendations on it
- Discuss, with the same exception, and make recommendations on any questions within the scope of the Charter or affecting the powers and functions of any organ of the United Nations
- Initiate studies and make recommendations to promote international political cooperation, the development and codification of international law, the realization of human rights and fundamental freedoms, and international collaboration in the economic, social, humanitarian, cultural, educational and health fields
- Make recommendations for the peaceful settlement of any situation that might impair friendly   relations among nations
- Receive and consider reports from the Security Council and other United Nations organs
- Consider and approve the United Nations budget and establish the financial assessments of   member states
- Elect the non-permanent members of the Security Council and the members of other United Nations councils and organs and, on the recommendation of the Security Council, appoint the Secretary-General.

Pursuant to its "Uniting for Peace" resolution of November 1950 (resolution 377 (V)), the General Assembly may act where the Security Council fails to act, owing to the negative vote of a permanent member, in a case where there appears to be a threat to the peace, breach of the peace or act of aggression.

The Assembly can consider the matter immediately with a view to making recommendations to Members for collective measures to maintain or restore international peace and security.

While the Assembly is empowered to make only non-binding recommendations to States on international issues within its competence, it has, nonetheless, initiated actions—political, economic, humanitarian, social and legal—which have affected the lives of millions of people throughout the world.

The landmark Millennium Declaration, adopted in 2000, and the 2005 World Summit Outcome Document reflect the commitment of Member States to reach specific goals to attain peace, security and disarmament along with development and poverty eradication; safeguard human rights and promote the rule of law; protect our common environment; meet the special needs of Africa; and strengthen the United Nations.

The search for consensus

Each Member State in the Assembly has one vote. Votes taken on designated important issues, such as recommendations on peace and security and the election of Security Council members, require a two-thirds majority of Member States, but other questions are decided by simple majority.

Functions and Powers of the Security Council

Under the United Nations Charter, the functions and powers of the Security Council are:

- to maintain international peace and security in accordance with the principles and purposes of the United Nations;
- to investigate any dispute or situation which might lead to international friction;
- to recommend methods of adjusting such disputes or the terms of settlement;
- to formulate plans for the establishment of a system to regulate armaments;
- to determine the existence of a threat to the peace or act of aggression and to recommend what action should be taken;
- to call on Members to apply economic sanctions and other measures not involving the use of force to prevent or stop aggression;
- to take military action against an aggressor;
- to recommend the admission of new Members;
- to exercise the trusteeship functions of the United Nations in "strategic areas";
- to recommend to the General Assembly the appointment of the Secretary-General and, together with the Assembly, to elect the Judges of the International Court of Justice.

Section 2

INDIA AT THE UNITED NATIONS

India maintains a close relationship with the United Nations. It has contributed significantly to the laying of the foundation to achieve equity and peace in the world.

What strengthens the India-UN relationship is the shared commitment to multilateralism and dialogue as the key for attaining shared goals of nations of the world.

India's resolve to address the common challenges faced by humankind including those related to peacekeeping, sustainable development, poverty eradication, environment, and climate change are in direct agreement with the Charter's goals.

India continues to collaborate with the UN on combating terrorism, disarmament, human rights, health and pandemic, migration, cyber security, space, and frontier technologies such as Artificial Intelligence. It has stood by and participated in the comprehensive reform of the United Nations, including the reform of the Security Council.

Indian Delegates arrive for United Nations Security Conference San Francisco: L to R; seated - Sir V.T. Krishnamachari, Representative of Indian States; Sir Ramaswami

India is a prime member of the UN and signed the **Declaration by the United Nations** at Washington on January 1, 1942. India took active part in the historic **UN Conference of International Organization** at San Francisco from April 25 to June 26, 1945.

As a founding member of the UN, India strongly backs the objectives and principles of the UN and has made notable contributions to executing the goals of the **UN Charter,** and the evolution of its specialized programs and agencies.

India strongly believes that the UN and the processes of international relations that it has fostered should remain the most efficient means for tackling today's global challenges. India is bound by its pledge and efforts to work with the committee of nations in the spirit of multilateralism to achieve comprehensive and equitable solutions to all problems troubling the peoples of the world including development and poverty eradication, climate change, terrorism, piracy, disarmament, peace building and peacekeeping, and human rights.

History of India's engagement with UN

Independent India (in 1947) viewed its membership at the United Nations as a certainty for maintaining international peace and security. India spearheaded the UN's tumultuous years of struggle against colonialism and apartheid (in South Africa).

India was the co-sponsor of the landmark **1960 Declaration** adopted by the UN on Granting of Independence to Colonial Countries and Peoples which proclaimed the need to unconditionally end colonialism in all its manifestations. India was also elected the first chair of the **Decolonization Committee** (Committee of 24) where its ceaseless efforts to put an end to colonialism. India was amongst the most outspoken detractors of apartheid and racial discrimination in South Africa.

In fact, India was the first country to raise the issue at the UN and played a pivotal role in the formation of a **Sub-Committee against Apartheid** set up by the General Assembly. When the **Convention on Elimination** of all forms of **Racial Discrimination** was adopted in 1965, India was among the earliest signatories.

India's stature as a founding member of the **Non-Aligned Movement** and the **Group of 77** cemented its position within the UN organization as a leading advocate of the concerns and aspirations of developing countries and the creation of a more

equitable international economic and political order.

Indians at United Nations

India was represented in the UN by some of its best women and men.

Arcot Ramasamy Mudaliar was India's delegate to the San Francisco Conference which led to the creation of the United Nations. He also had the honour of serving as the first President of the United **Nations Economic and Social Council** in 1946.

India & The United Nations

Hansa Mehta represented India on the **Sub-Committee on the Status of Women** in 1946. As the Indian delegate on the UN Human Rights Commission in 1947–48, she was responsible for changing the language of the **Universal Declaration of Human Rights** from "all men are created equal" to "all human beings", highlighting the need for gender equality.

Lakshmi Menon, India's delegate to the Third Committee in 1948, argued forcefully in favour of non-discrimination based on sex and "the equal rights of men and women" in the in the Universal Declaration of Human Rights. A strong advocate of the "universality" of human rights, she argued that "if women and people under colonial rule were not explicitly mentioned in the Universal Declaration, they would not be considered included in "everyone".

Mrs. Vijaya Lakshmi Pandit had the distinction of being the first woman to be elected President of the United Nations General Assembly in 1953.

Chinmaya Rajaninath Gharekhan served as ECOSOC President in 1990. In January 1993 was appointed by the UN Secretary General as a special envoy to the Middle East peace process in the capacity of Under-Secretary- General of the United Nations, a position he held until 1999.

1947 - 1956 P. S. Lokanathan (India) Executive Secretary, UNESCAP

1956-1967: Binay Ranjan Sen Director General of the FAO

1965-1967: Manohar Balaji Sarwate, Secretary-General, ITU

1956 - 1959 Chakravarthi V. Narasimhan, Executive Secretary of UNESCAP

1968: Sushil K. Dev (India) Acting Executive Director, World Food Programme

1978-1992: Arcot Ramachandran, Executive Director of UN- Habitat

1974-1989: Chandrika Prasad Srivastava, Secretary-General of the International Maritime Organization (IMO)

1979-1981: Padinjarethalakal Cherian Alexander, Executive Director, Int'l Trade Centre

1985-1988: Judge Nagendra Singh, President of the International Court of Justice

2009-2012: Judge Kamaljit Singh Garewal, Judge on the UN Appeals Tribunal (UNAT)

India & The United Nations

Currently there are seven Indians in senior leadership positions at the United Nations   at the levels of Under Secretary General and Assistant Secretary General.

Mr. Atul Khare, Under-Secretary-General, Dpt. of Operational Support

Anita Bhatia, Assistant Secretary-General & Deputy Executive Director of the UN Women

Mr. Chandramouli Ramanathan, Assistant Secretary-General, Dept of Mgt Strategy, Policy & Compliance

Mr. Nikhil Seth, ASG & Executive Director, UNITAR

Mr. Satya S. Tripathi, ASG, UNEP

Lt General Shailesh Tinaikar, Force Commander, UNMISS

Judge Dalveer Bhandari, Judge, ICJ

Mr. Ovais Sarmad, ASG & Deputy Executive Secretary, UNFCC

UN Committees

The First Committee

The First Committee is devoted to non-proliferation. India has joined many multilateral export control treaties. To address global concerns of proliferation of armaments and their sale to terrorists, India has been a party to the consensus and resolution on Measures to Prevent Terrorists from Acquiring Weapons of Mass Destruction (WMD).

India is committed to the goal of creating a nuclear weapon free world and total exclusion of nuclear weapons. It believes that this objective can be fulfilled through a gradual and comprehensive process underwritten by a collective commitment and a global and non-discriminatory multi-party framework. This is outlined in India's Working Paper on Nuclear Disarmament submitted to the UN General Assembly (UNGA) in 2006.

India is aligned to the Chemical Weapons Convention (CWC) which enunciates the global testament against the use of chemical weapons. It has been India's permanent position that the use of chemical weapons anywhere, at any time, by anybody under any circumstances, cannot be justified. India believes that the perpetrators of such acts must be held guilty of war crimes. Though the convention is faced with serious challenges at this time, India is unflinching in its credibility and integrity.

India remains resistant to the weaponization of outer space. It has not, and will not, resort to any arms race in space. It has been a consistent advocate of conserving space as a common heritage of all humankind. India states that space should remain solely for science, and an ever-expansive frontier for collaborative endeavors of all space-faring nations.

India propagates reasonable underwriting of the prevention of an arms race in space within the multi-ended framework of the UN. She is committed to the discourse of a legally-binding instrument on arms race prevention in outer space to be negotiated in the Conference on Disarmament. This instrument was pending ratification since 1982. India has been an active contributor in the Group of Governmental Experts on the Prevention of an Arms Race in Outer Space which concluded its session in March 2019. India also participated in dialogue on Transparency and Confidence-Building. Measures (TCBM) for space security.

At the 73rd session of the First Committee in 2018, India voted in favor of all resolutions submitted under the Outer Space Cluster, including the prevention of an arms race in outer space (which India also co-sponsored). On pragmatic measures to be implemented for such prevention (No First Placement) India remains resolute. (Discussed in detail in the following pages)

The Role of Science and Technology in the context of International Security and Disarmament

This issue was first added to the agenda of the First Committee in 1988, and India was the main sponsor. By introducing a draft resolution, the Indian delegate iterated India's growing concerns on large amounts of resources being devoted to developing new weapon systems and the resultant uncertainty and insecurity among member nations.

Advanced use of nuclear explosive power, miniaturization and large-scale computing capabilities using micro-electronics, and fuel and laser technology are threatening world peace. India argued for developing a shared perception of international security. On December 7, 1988, the first resolution on the issue, (43/77A) was adopted with a record vote of 129 in favour, seven against (with 14 abstentions).

Since 2017, India has been presenting the resolution on the Role of Science and Technology in the Context of International Security and Disarmament. This has been adopted by consensus and attracted co-sponsors across the globe. The resolution had mandated the UN Secretary General to submit a report on the current developments in science and technology and their potential impact on international security and disarmament efforts.

India remains resolute in playing a leading and substantive role together with other partner nations, in deliberations on prevention of an arms race in space, including legally binding measures, TCBMs and long-term sustainability guidelines.

Second Committee: Economic & Financial

The Second Committee concerns itself with issues of economic growth and development.

It addresses macroeconomic policy; development financing; sustainable development; human settlements; globalization and interdependence; poverty eradication; operational activities for development; agriculture.

(Picture: Mr. I.S. Chadha of India (first from right) at the Second Committee meeting on the World Economic Situation. Source: UN Archives)

development, food security and nutrition; information and communications technologies for development and global partnerships.

India presented its Voluntary National Review Report on Implementation of Sustainable Development Goals (SDGs) at a United Nations high-level political forum on sustainable development in 2017. India highlighted that apart from integrating the SDGs into its on-going   national and sub-national policies and programs, India will continue to focus on nurturing partnerships at the regional and global levels.

In 2020, 50 countries (27 first time presenters, and 23 second time presenters) conducted Voluntary National Reviews (VNR) at the High-Level Political Forum (HPLF). India was among the nations that presented its VNR for the second time (first time in 2017).

India has consistently articulated its support to a multilateral trading system and the centrality of the World Trade Organization (WTO) as the foundation of a rule-based, open, transparent, non-discriminatory, and inclusive multilateral trading framework with sustainable development at the core of its agenda. India has emphasized that the institutional reform of agencies like the International Monetary Fund (IMF) should be a priority to better cater to the interests of the developing nations.

India saliently contributed to the debates and discussions that led to

the adoption of the Global Compact on Safe, Orderly and Regular Migration. India believes that safe, orderly, and regular migration helps in fulfillment of SDGs which will in turn assist in the achievement of SDGs. The move will assure that migration will be a question of choice and not compulsion.

Third Committee: Social, Humanitarian & Cultural

The Third Committee deals with a variety of social, humanitarian, and human rights issues that affect people across the world. The committee discusses challenges relating to the advancement of women and levelling of gender inequalities. It concerns itself with child protection, indigenous problems, refugee rehabilitation, and fundamental freedom guarantees.

It is committed to eliminate racism and racial discrimination and establish the right to self- determination. Also in focus are social development issues including that of youth and family. It addresses issues pertaining to senior citizens, and persons with disabilities, prevention of crime, criminal justice, and international narcotics control.

On behalf of India, at the first session of the Commission of Human Rights in 1947, while drafting the Universal Declaration of the Human Rights (UDHR), Dr Hansa Mehta, a bold and avant garde social activist, ensuredthat the first Article of the UDHR iterated 'all human beings' rather than 'all men being free and equal'.

India has consistently stressed that true human rights cannot be achieved by undertaking aggressive and overly micro-managing methods sans the consultation and consent of the member nation. Such a 'confrontational approach'   is counterproductive and ends in 'politicization' of human rights. India believes in only dialogue, consultation and cooperation with non-selectivity and transparency as guiding principles in tackling human rights issues.

India has partnered with UN Women from the day of its inception. To address mission-critical questions of gender equality and women empowerment in the national and global context, India has so   far made a voluntary contribution of US$ 8 million to UN Women for its global operations. India facilitated the field visit of the UN-Women Executive Board Bureau to India in 2017 which provided an opportunity for the UN Women delegation to gain a true and first-hand understanding of UN-Women's work at the national level.

Fourth Committee: Special Political & Decolonization

The Fourth Committee ponders over a broad range of issues related to decolonization, nuclear radiation, peacekeeping operations, special political missions, and the United Nations Relief and Works Agency (UNRWA) for Palestinian Refugees in the near East. The Report of the Special Committee on Israeli Practices was submitted to the UNGA. The committee also deliberates on the agenda on assistance in landmine action, and university for peace biennially and triennially.

Having once been colonized, India is perpetually at the battle-front against colonialism and racial discrimination like apartheid. India was, naturally, involved with the organization of the historic Afro-Asian Conference at Bandung, Indonesia, in 1955.

Five years later, India was the co-sponsor of the landmark 1960 Declaration on the Granting of Independence to Colonial Countries and Peoples, which was adopted by the General Assembly. The declaration proclaimed the need to unconditionally end colonialism in all its manifestations.

India trusts that adopting a practical approach towards decolonization would lead to   attainment of the legitimate aspirations of the people of 17 Non-Self-Governing Territories. India has abided by the demand for stepped-up efforts to see this cumbersome process to its logical end.

UNCOPUOS

India has backed efforts to build mutual trust and confidence through the discussions on Long Term Sustainability of Outer Space activities at UN Committee on the Peaceful Uses of Outer Space (UNCOPUOS). India has also rallied for substantive consideration of the issue of Prevention of Arms Race (PAROS) at the Conference on Disarmament. Itshas also been actively engaged in capacity building in space law, by hosting several national and international workshops and seminars on outer space issues.

In 2017, India hosted the 24th session of the Asia Pacific Regional Space Agency Forum (APRSAF) with the concept --'Space Technology for Enhanced Governance and Development' in Bengaluru. The same year, India hosted the 38th Asian Conference of Remote Sensing with the theme 'Space Applications: Touching Human Lives' in New Delhi.

In June 2018, India hosted the 46th Plenary of the Coordination Group on Meteorological Satellites (CGMS). The Indian Space Research Organisation (ISRO) based out of Bengaluru, shares its facilities and expertise through the UN-affiliated Centre for Space Science and Technology Education in Asia and the Pacific (CSSTEAP) based in Dehradun. There have been over 1,600 participants from over 50 countries.

Fifth Committee: Administrative & Budgetary

The Fifth Committee considers and approves the budget of the United Nations. It also considers and approves financial and budgetary arrangements with specialized agencies and makes recommendations to agencies. It is empowered to consider urgent matters relating to the financing of a peacekeeping mission authorized by the Security Council at any of its sessions.

India has stressed that resource allocation should be commensurate with our collective onus in realizing Agenda 2030. The UN mechanism has to be adequately resourced to serve member states in achieving goals. The imperative of 'doing more with less', and rationalization of resources should not underplay UN's abilities.

The UN system must be robust enough to deliver its mandate. India has backed delegation of authority to field-level managers, aligning authority with accountability and changing organizational strategy. India's share of the UN's budget has been increasing recently. This includes a 13 per cent increase from 2019 in its assessment rates. India is among a few countries which have been paying all assessments in full and on time, including peacekeeping contributions.

India is among member states that continue to be owed significant sums towards troop and contingent owned equipment (COE) reimbursements from active peacekeeping missions. It has   emphasized that these arrears and recurrent delay in reimbursement have turned Troop Contributing Countries (TCCs) into de-facto financiers of UN peacekeeping. This has become an involuntary contribution and is beyond many TCCs' capacity to pay. As per latest figures, as of September 2020, US$ 357 million was owed to member nations for troops and police units, as compared to US$ 6 million last year.

The emergent liquidity crisis in the regular budget is a cause for concern. While the cash position has improved slightly as compared to the previous years. This can be attributed primarily to 'belt-tightening measures' such as hiring freeze, and lower spending due to COVID-19.

COVID-19 pandemic, and its rapid spread to populations across the world remains a challenge in the 75th session of the General Assembly and for the working of the Fifth Committee. India has proactively engaged in the deliberations of this session on both the Proposed Program Plan and Programme Budget for 2021.

India, continually and actively, intends to participate in the committee's deliberations on other agenda items, that include review of the implementation of the peace and security pillar reform, implementation of resolution 72/266B, construction and property management, funding model of the Department of Management Strategy, Policy and Compliance (DMSPC) and Department of Operational Support (DOS).

India will also push hard for the review of budgetary cycle involving the Committee for Program Coordination (CPC), Advisory Committee on Administrative and Budgetary Questions (ACABQ), United Nations Common System, Pension System, Umoja and Administration of Justice.

Close attention will be paid to the deliberations on the Scale of Assessments, the Capital Master Plan, all program budget implications and revised estimates, Improving the Financial Situation of the United   Nations, and reports of the Board of Auditors and the Office of Internal Oversight Services (OIOS)

Stocks Convention 1995, MARPOL 73/78, the International Ballast Water (Source: UN Archives) Pic: On left, Sixth Committee expert Mr. Akbar Ali Khan (India), 1953

The Sixth Committee is the primary forum for the consideration of legal questions in the General Assembly. India is an enthusiastic participant in the multination efforts at developing collective management of ocean affairs and one of the early parties to the 1982 UN Convention on the Law of the Sea (UNCLOS).

India is a signatory to the agreement on implementation of Part XI of the Convention of 10 December 1982, Fish Convention 2004 that prevents invasive aquatic alien species, London Convention 1972, and other pacts that govern various activities of the oceans, especially the conservation and sustainable use of aquatic resources.

India is continually and proactively engaged in deliberations and collaboration towards developing international instruments concerning over-exploitation and destruction of marine resources. The marine Biodiversity Beyond National Jurisdiction (BBNJ) and Global Geospatial Information Management (GGIM) are two of India's favourite pursuits in the field of marine resources conservation.

India played an emphatic role in the first Cycle of the Regular Process during 2010-2015, which culminated in the First Global Integrated Marine Assessment on the state of the health of oceans. India has taken part in the second cycle of the Regular Process (2017 – 2020) and participated in the preparation of a Second World Ocean Assessment and Regular Process support to other ongoing ocean-related processes. India has demonstrated its expertise in the area of marine chemistry, physical oceanography, marine geology, and marine biology.

We continue to make fruitful attempts to bring our national laws in sync with our international obligations. India is a party to the Paris Agreement on Climate Change under United Nations Framework Convention on Climate Change (UNFCCC), and Doha Amendment to the Kyoto Protocol.

India has acceded to the UN Customs Convention on International Transport Goods under Transport International Routier (TIR) Carnets and signed the UN (Singapore) Convention on International Settlement Agreements Resulting from Mediation.

Recently, India has enacted nearly 43 new acts, ranging from legislations on mental health, rights of persons with disabilities, civil aviation, labour and employment, agriculture and farmer welfare, Goods and Services Tax (GST), national waterways, and anti-hijacking.

India is an active member of the United Nations Commission on International Trade Laws (UNCITRAL) since inception and plays an effective role in all six working groups. India is a party to UNCITRAL Model Law on International Commercial Arbitration and the New York Convention on the Recognition and Enforcement of Foreign Arbitral Awards (New York Convention).

These agreements provide the basis for contracting states to enact domestic laws and implement cross-border arbitration system. India has adopted, to a considerable extent, the UNCITRAL Model Law through the Indian Arbitration and Conciliation   Act of 1996 (the Arbitration Act). She has been contributing to the Residual Special Court for Sierra Leone and enable the Court to carry out its functions effectively.

UN's Diamond Jubilee

The United Nations celebrated its 75th anniversary (and its founding charter also) in 2020. What should have been a celebratory event was marked by a time of devastation for the world caused by increasing terrorism and compounded by a major health crisis caused by the Covid-19 epidemic. These events created deep economic and social setbacks to humankind as whole.

Several planned modalities of the commemoration, agreed to by member states in 2019, had to be altered and rendered virtual because of prohibitions cramping international travel and face to face meetings. Many of the events were held in hybrid format (partly online and partly offline)

The UN marked the occasion with a High-Level Meeting of the 75th UN General Assembly on September 21, 2020 on the theme 'The Future We Want, the UN We Need: Reaffirming our Collective Commitment to Multilateralism'. In his intervention, Indian Prime Minister Narendra Modi stressed the need for reformed multilateralism reflecting today's realities. He called for initiatives that give voice to all stakeholders, addresses contemporary challenges and focuses on human welfare. During this meeting, world leaders also adopted the UN@75 Political Declaration commemorating 75 years of the UN.

Other commemorative events included observance ceremonies to mark the 75th anniversary of the signing of the UN Charter (June, 26, 2020) and to mark the 75th UN Day (October 24, 2020). A special UN@75 Virtual Youth Plenary was also organised on 9 September 2020.

                                                India & The United Nations

The 75th session of the UN General Assembly opened on September 15, 2020, with Ambassador Volkan Bozkir of Turkey as President. Upon taking office, the new president emphasized that in his term, his priorities will be:

- Fighting COVID-19 together
- Celebrating 75 years of the UN
- Recommitting to and strengthening multilateralism
- Advancing humanitarian agenda with a focus on the most vulnerable
- Taking action to achieve the 2030 Agenda and SDGs
- Promoting Gender Equality

Addressing the General Assembly (through a pre-recorded message) in the General Debate on September 26, 2020, PM Narendra Modi called for urgent reform of the UN and inclusion of India's voice in decision-making structures. He also outlined India's contribution to the global response to COVID-19, and announced that India   will make available its vaccine supply and delivery capacities to the rest of the world,   in keeping with its philosophy of seeing the world as one family (Vasudaiva Kutumbam)

Other UN@75 initiatives in January 2020

The United Nations also launched a "global conversation" to mark its 75th anniversary. Through ongoing surveys and informal dialogues with multiple stakeholders including civil society, youth and women, this initiative seeks to understand peoples' expectations of international cooperation and the UN in particular.

It is also the biggest survey so far on priorities for recovering from   COVID-19. Early outcomes indicate that amid COVID-19, the immediate priority of most respondents is improved access to basic healthcare services, and growing support for tackling poverty, inequalities and combating unemployment.

Representation in UN Bodies

India has seamlessly and successfully run for elections to various UN bodies. She has won several major polls in the last few years including those to the Human Right Council (HRC), Economic and Social Council (ECOSOC), and International Narcotics Control Board.

Judge Dalveer Bhandari's election to International Court of Justice (ICJ), Preeti Saran's election to Committee on Economic, Social and Cultural Rights (CESCR), Dr. Neeru Chadha's election to International Tribunal for the Law of the Sea (ITLOS), Dr. Aniruddha Rajput's election to International Law Commission (ILC), Ambassador P. Gopinathan's election to Joint Inspection Unit (JIU), are other successful representations in the UN system.

Currently India is represented in the following 23 UN Bodies whose elections are held at   United Nations headquarters in New York.

1.	United Nations Commission on International Trade Law (UNCITRAL)	2016-2022
2.	International Seabed Authority (ISA) Council	2017-2020
3.	Legal and Technical Commission of the ISA	2017-2021
4.	Finance Committee of ISA	2017-2021
5.	International Law Commission (ILC) - Dr. Aniruddha Rajput	2017-2021
6.	Economic and Social Council (ECOSOC)	2018-2020
7.	International Court of Justice (ICJ) - Judge Dalveer Bhandari	2018-2026
8.	Joint Inspection Unit (JIU) - Ambassador. P. Gopinathan	2018-2022
9.	Commission on Population and Development (CPD)	2018-2021
10.	Commission for Social Development (CSocD)	2018-2021
11.	Commission on Narcotic Drugs (CND)	2018-2021
12.	Human Rights Council (HRC)	2019-2021
13.	Committee on Economic, Social and Cultural Rights (CESCR) - Ambassador Preeti Saran	2019-2022
14.	Committee on Non-Governmental Organizations (CNGO)	2019-2022
15.	Executive Board of UNDP/UNFPA/UNOPS	2019-2021
16.	Executive Board of UN-Women	2019-2021
17.	Commission on Crime Prevention and Criminal Justice (CCPCJ)	2019-2021
18.	Programme Coordination Committee of UN AIDS Executive Board	2020-2022
19.	International Narcotics Control Board (INCB) - Ms. Jagjit Pavadia	2020-2025
20.	Committee for Programme and Coordination (CPC)	2021-23
21.	Commission on the Status of Women	2021-25
22.	Commission on Population and Development	2021-25
23.	Advisory	Committee

Familiarization visits to India

India has been engaging closely with the global community at the United Nations by promoting familiarization visits to India by ambassadors and permanent representatives of various member states represented at the United Nations.

In the last two years, UN ambassadors of over 50 countries have visited India to get a better comprehension and ringside view of India's growth dynamics, vibrant democracy, developments in science and technology, including atomic energy and space exploration.

Significant Achievements by India at the UN (Annexure-1)

Major Initiatives:

- UNGA resolution declaring June 21 as the International Day of Yoga was adopted in December 2014 with a record number of 177 co-sponsors. This adoption fast-tracked global observance of International Yoga Day.

- Hindi usage in UN public communications (UN News, Weekly Audio Bulletins on UN Radio and UN Social Media) began in March 2018 following the MoU signed by the UN.

- The first ever single-country South-South cooperation initiative at the UN was launched in June 2017 through the "India-UN Development Partnership Fund", a USD 100 million fund facility to undertake projects across the developing world. In April 2018, a USD 50 million Commonwealth window was created under the fund to support SDG-related projects in developing Commonwealth countries.

- Following efforts made in three previous attempts (2009, 2016 and 2017), the Security Council finally on May 1, 2019 approved the addition of Masood Azhar to the 1267 sanctions of individuals and entities subject to the assets freeze, travel ban and arms embargo.

Elections

India is one of the few countries whose candidates have won every election at the UN in New York.

- The election of Judge Dalveer Bhandari to the International Court of Justice (ICJ) in Nov 2017 was a landmark event for India in terms of its unprecedented success in unseating a sitting judge from UK, a P5 member.

- Dr. Neeru Chadha became the first Indian woman to be elected in June 2017 as Judge of the International Tribunal for the Law of the Sea (ITLOS) for the period 2017-2026.

- Dr. Aniruddha Rajput was elected to the International Law Commission (ILC) in Nov 2016 for the term 2017-2021 with highest number of votes (Total of 160 out of 193 votes) in the Asia-Pacific Group.

- India was elected to the Human Rights Council in Oct 2018 for the period 2019- 2022 with highest number of votes (188/193).

- Jagjit Pavadia was re-elected as Member to the International Narcotics Control Board (INCB) on May 7, 2019 for the term 2020-25 with the highest number of votes (44 out of the 54-member ECOSOC).

- On 15 Sept 2020, India was elected to the Commission of the Status of Women by the ECOSOC. India secured 38 out 54 votes polled. India's tenure on the CSW will   last from 2021 to 2025. India was also elected to the Committee for Program and Coordination (CPC) and Commission on Population and Development.

- Vidisha Maitra was elected to the Advisory Committee on Administrative and Budgetary Questions by vote of the General Assembly. She won the highest number of votes - 126 out of the 192 valid votes (with 2 abstentions).

Other achievements/participation in important events

- In Nov 2017, a voluntary compact was reached between UN Secretary-General and the Indian government on commitment to eliminate sexual exploitation and abuse in peacekeeping, humanitarian and development work. Indian PM Modi joined the Circle of Leadership on the prevention of and response to sexual exploitation and abuse in United Nations operations

- In Sept 2018, UNEP recognized PM Modi in the "Policy Leadership" category for pioneering work in championing the International Solar Alliance and for the pledge to eliminate single-use plastic in India by 2022. UNEP also selected   Cochin International Airport (fully-powered by solar energy) for the Champion for Entrepreneurial Vision Award.

- International Solar Alliance (ISA) was registered with the UN as a treaty-based inter-governmental organization from February 9, 2018.

- India ratified the Paris Agreement and Second Commitment Period of Kyoto Protocol in Climate Change in August 2017.

- UNGA adopted a resolution in December 2014 on recognizing Indian festivals--Diwali, Buddha Purnima and Gurpurab by the UN. The first official celebration of Diwali at UN Headquarters took place in 2016.

- First reference to 'Yoga' was made in September 2018 in the Political Declaration on Non-Communicable Diseases, a health-related resolution in UNGA.

- India was among the 40 plus countries in 2017 that presented their Voluntary National Review at the UN on the progress made in achievement of SDGs. India presented its second VNR virtually at the 2020 HLPF on July 13, 2020. Vice Chairman of NITI Aayog Rajiv Kumar presented India's VNR. India's commitment to the SDGs was presented by highlighting our national development   agenda as reflected in the motto of "Sabka Saath Sabka Vikaas" (Collective Efforts for Inclusive Growth).

- In November 2018, India successfully operationalized the co-deployment of 120 troops from Kazakhstan as part of its contingent in UN Interim Force in Lebanon (UNIFIL).   India also initiated the process of deployment of a mixed Formed Police Unit to UN Mission in South Sudan.

- India's contribution to the Voluntary Trust Fund of the UN Tax Committee (that promotes the participation of developing countries in the work of

UN committee on   tax matters and looks at key issues that can mobilize resources for sustainable development) was recognized in UNGA Resolution of September 2017.

- UN Day concert (featuring Sarod Maestro Ustad Amjad Ali Khan) organized on Oct 24, 2018 after a gap of 52 years under the theme, "Traditions of Peace and Non- Violence".

- On September 24, 2019, India commemorated the 150th birth anniversary of Mahatma Gandhi by holding a high-level event at the UN. The event was hosted by PM Modi in which the UNSG Antonio Guterres, President of South Korea Moon Jae In, Prime Minister of Bangladesh Sheikh Hasina, Prime Minister of New Zealand Jessica Arden, and Prime Minister of Jamaica Andrew Holness took part.

- United Nations Postal Administration (UNPA) brought out the following four postal   stamps in collaboration with the Mission:

1. Personalized stamp sheet on birth centenary and golden jubilee of noted singer M.S. Subbulakshmi's 50th anniversary performance at the UN

2. Special commemorative stamp sheet on International Day of Yoga (iii) Special commemorative stamp sheet on Diwali

3. Special commemorative stamp on the 150th birth anniversary of Mahatma Gandhi.

- PM Modi delivered a virtual keynote address at the High- Level Segment of the ECOSOC on July 17, 2020. The theme of the session was "Multilateralism after COVID 19: What kind of UN do we need at the 75th anniversary?". PM Modi, in his remarks highlighted many aspects related to India's commitment to achieve the SDGs and actions taken to combat COVID-19.

- PM Modi batted for reformed multilateralism and human-centric globalization

- PM Modi delivered his virtual address at the UN on September 21, 2020 on the occasion of the 75th anniversary of the UN. He also delivered India's national statement at the 75th UNGA General Debate on Sept 26 2020. In his General Debate speech, Modi said "A fragmented world is in the interest of no one". He added: "In this new era, we will have to give a new direction to multilateralism,   and to the United Nations".

- PM Modi spoke virtually at the Climate Ambition Summit on December 21, 2020. He pledged that by 2047, centenarian India would exceed the world's expectations in implementing counters to climate change. He said: "On the occasion of the 5th anniversary of the Paris Agreement the world should not lose sight of historical emissions". He called for a review of actions taken by all countries   based on the commitments they had made under the agreement.

Section 3

UN Women

War, violent conflicts and terrorism leave a devastating effect on women and girls. There is also strong evidence to suggest that women's participation in peace processes contributes to longer, and more resilient peace after conflict. Empowering women fuels thriving economies, spurring productivity and growth. Yet gender inequalities remain deeply entrenched in every society.

For many years, however, the United Nations battled numerous challenges in its efforts to promote women empowerment. The international body lacked a single, focussed driver to direct UN activities on issues pertaining to gender equality.

In July 2010, the United Nations General Assembly created UN Women, the United Nations entity for Gender Equality and the Empowerment of Women, to address such challenges. A global champion for women and girls, UN Women was established to accelerate progress on meeting their needs worldwide.

UN Women supports UN Member States as they set global standards for achieving gender equality, and works with governments and civil society to design laws, policies, programmes and services needed to ensure that the standards are effectively implemented and truly benefit women and girls worldwide. It works globally to make the vision of the Sustainable Development Goals a reality for women and girls. It focuses on four strategic priorities:

- Women lead, participate in and benefit equally from governance systems
- Women have income security, decent work and economic autonomy
- All women and girls live a life free from all forms of violence
- Women and girls contribute to and have greater influence in building sustainable peace and resilience, and benefit equally from the prevention of natural disasters and conflicts and humanitarian action.

With this as the backdrop, UN Women's main roles are:

- To support inter-governmental bodies, such as the Commission on the Status of Women, in their formulation of policies, global standards and norms.

- To help Member States implement these standards, standing ready to provide suitable technical and financial support to those countries that request it, and to forge effective partnerships with civil society.

- To lead and coordinate the UN system's work on gender equality, as well as promote accountability, including through regular monitoring of system-wide progress.

UN Women in Peace and Security

UN Women supports women's full and equal representation and participation in all levels of peace processes and security efforts. UN Women's work on women, peace, and security is guided by 10 UN Security Council resolutions—1325, 1820, 1888, 1889, 1960, 2106, 2122, 2242, 2467, and 2493—and is bolstered by a number of related normative frameworks, which make up the broader women, peace, and security (WPS) agenda.

UN Women leads on implementing the WPS agenda through research initiatives, data collection, learning exchanges, and documentation of good practices to inform policy and programming. Our resources and publications provide knowledge and guidance for ensuring women's participation and inclusion in all aspects of peace processes.

In the current global peace and security context, with many new and emerging threats from violent extremism, climate change, prolonged violent conflict, human trafficking, and unprecedented and protracted refugee and humanitarian crises, UN Women's efforts to implement the women, peace, and security agenda assume critical importance.

WOMEN AT THE UN

Countless women across the globe are striving to avoid conflict, rehabilitate people who have faced crisis, and build lasting peace, often putting their own lives at risk.

This is the story of 14 women world over who have negotiated with extremists, taken part in peace talks, advanced political solutions, advocated women's rights and participation in government, built social support ecosystems, and brought about peaceful transitions. Their stories originate in the Central African Republic, the Democratic Republic of the Congo, Mali, South Sudan, Sudan, Lebanon, Yemen, and Colombia.

A Security Council debate on Women, Peace and Security, was held in October in New York, and December in Seoul, Republic of Korea, at the Peacekeeping Ministerial. This was a conference designed to gather political support for peacekeeping operations from the international community, identify new interventions to be implemented to strengthen peacekeeping operations and evaluate the implementation of such operations.

Zekia Mussa, Youth Activist, South Sudan

Zekia Musa is a 29-year-old visually impaired youth activist and peacebuilder who works with the South Sudanese Ministry of General Education and Instruction representing people with disabilities. She also mentors disabled pupils at schools in the capital Juba.

Photo by Maura Ajak/Copyright © UN

"Inequalities are rife across South Sudan. We must enact equal laws and justice for everybody. Disabled people need to be included in decision-making that impact us directly. I advocate for our rights because I want to see us being included and heard in the future of our country," says Zekia Musa.

Fifi Baka, Human Rights Activist, Democratic Republic of the Congo Photo by Ley Uwera/Copyright © UN

As executive secretary of the Gender and Women's Rights Network, Fifi Baka advocates protection of women and girl children fundamental rights.

In the Congo capital Kinshasa, she also represents the Nothing Without Women Movement (Rien sans les Femmes/RSLF), which unites over 300 civil society NGOs and Congolese activists to promote equal participation of women in decision-making bodies across the republic.

"I am convinced that until women are not adequately regarded and participative in major decision-making and peace negotiations, we will not have peace or sustainable development in our country," declares Fifa Baka.

Loda Coulibaly, Activist, Mali Photo by Kani Sissoko/Copyright © UN

Loda Coulibaly is engaged in advancing women and girl child fundamental rights in Mali as a member of several women's NGOs including the Network of Young Women Leaders of Political Parties and Civil Society and the G5 Sahel Women's Coordination Group. Loda demands participation of women in the peace process in Mali and is a member of the Citizen Initiative for the Consolidation of Peace and Women's Political Leadership project.

"Women play an exceptionally significant role in society. I advocate the participation of women in the ongoing transitional process in Mali," says Loda Coulibaly.

Béatrice Epaye, Member of Parliament, Central African Republic Photo by Leila Thiam/Copyright © UN

Béatrice Epaye has been elected many times as a member of parliament representing Markonda, her home constituency. She has utilized her position as President of the Forum of Women Parliamentarians to reform the country's poll code, making it more salubrious to women, by ensuring a 35 per cent quota of representation in government and elections.

"When we leverage the power of women in governance, we are bound to establish peace in my country. It is a woman's right to sit at the decision-making tables, not just around them. The last few elections have shown this is possible though we have a long way to go before we are adequately involved in critical decision-making," says Beatrice Epaye.

Olla al Sakkaf (27) is a youth campaigner from Yemen. After graduating from the Faculty of Arts at Taiz University, she enlisted with a civil society movement and a pioneer youth organization. She is engaged in projects relating to gender-based hate and violence, peacebuilding and improving the co-existence between communities.

"Wars have ravaged my country and demolished all hope for peace. Our lives are lived tragically. My intentions are to work towards the preservation of peace for future generations. Even a small change in this direction gives me hope for a better future…especially for women and youth of the country," says Olla al Sakkaf.

Randa Abu Salih is a Tyre Municipal Council member (Southern Lebanon) and chairs the Council's Women and Child Affairs Committee where she trains local police officers on women's rights and child abuse deterrence in some of the poorest areas of the city.

"I think Lebanese women face formidable challenges and we need to make sure all women are guaranteed their fundamental rights and are enabled to effectively participate in decision-making. We need to ensure that equitable justice is delivered to all women and children of the country," says Randa Abu Salih.

Ola al-Aghbary is a Yemeni 'community entrepreneur' who engages with several local and global organizations to achieve her goals. She is the Founder and Executive Director of the Sheba Youth Foundation for Development.

"I am hopeful that Yemeni women and youth of the country can restore peace in my country. We need to bring home our youth from the frontlines of war and hope that someday the roads will open and allow free movement of people. I do hope and believe that someday women will assume leadership positions and possess more influence and say in the running of the country," utters Ola al-Aghbary.

Hawa Games Dahab, Gender Specialist, Sudan

Photo by Maimana El Hassan/Copyright © UN

Hawa Games Dahab Gabjenda has wide-ranging experience as a gender specialist. She has campaigned for women's empowerment, development, humanitarian, and peacebuilding movements. She participated as a gender observer in the Juba peace talks held between the Transitional Government and the Sudan People's Liberation Movement in 2021.

"My allegiance and love for my community has driven my fight for peace. We must not forget where we come from. Peace is the most needed and valuable asset for any society that requires to be rebuilt after destruction by war and natural disasters. Peace should not be relegated to table conferences and mundane meetings and speeches in lofty halls. It should be restored on the streets filled with violence and mayhem," Hawa Games Dahab advocates sternly.

Alokiir Malual, Pioneer for Women's Participation, South Sudan

Photo by Maura Ajak/Copyright © UN

Alokiir Malual created history as the only woman to have endorsed a peace agreement in South Sudan in 2015. With UN support (in South Sudan), Alokiir was among the seven women signatories to the Revitalized Peace Agreement in September 2018. Now, she is part of the Revitalized Joint Monitoring and Evaluation Commission, set up to monitor and supervise the workings of the Revitalized Peace Agreement, and she also co-chairs the subcommittee on peacebuilding.

"We have opportunistically taken advantage of the peace process, to assure more participation for women. We achieved a 35 per cent quota in participative governance by forming women groups and campaigning for women's voice in government. We have leveraged our one position: one demand formula. This is an exemplary achievement by the South Sudanese women," asserts Alokiir Malual.

India & The United Nations

Sudanese campaigner Maha Zeinelabdin Abdelwahad Sidahmed spearheaded the Women of Sudanese Civic and Political Groups, better known as MANSAM. This, is an alliance of eight political women's groups and NGOs. During the Sudanese revolution in 2019, Maha was one among gender observers at the Juba peace talks held during the Transitional Government and the Sudan People's Liberation Movement in Juba in 2021.

"I impressed upon the Transitional Government and the opposing Sudan People's Liberation Movement-North to ensure that women participate actively in peace talks and promote implementation of the peace accord; Especially on security because it is vital to maintain peace," says Maha Zeinelabdin Abdelwahad Sidahmed.

In 1993, Victoria Sandino Simanca Herrera entered the Revolutionary Armed Forces of Colombia — People's Army (FARC-EP). Nearly 20 years later, she led the gender sub-commission on behalf of the FARC-EP at the Havana, Cuba, peace talks. In 2017, Victoria participated in the political council of the Fuerza Alternativa Revolucionaria del Común (FARC) party as one of the few women elected.

"I wish to participate actively in the change to be brought about in my country. War and violence must end. We have transformed into a different Colombia; one in which peace, social justice and equal rights for women are present," says Victoria Sandino

Mouna Awata is the head of the Women's Peace Hut (Case de la Paix) in Gao, which is supported by UN Women and the UN peace operation there (MINUSMA).

The Hut unites 76 women's movements from diverse ethnic and religious communities. Together, they act for

peace and social cohesion. Their aim is to prevent and resolve conflicts in this restive region of Mali. The Hut's scope of work includes mediating with armed groups, preventing violent extremism and working with survivors of sexual violence.

"Because of strife, all our men left Gao. Women were left behind on their own. So, we decided to form the Peace Hut where everybody is represented: Arab, Tamasheq, and Fulani women. We welcome everybody. This forum has helped us overcome challenges and differences," says Mouna Awata Touré.

Marthe Mbita, Peacebuilder, Central African Republic

Marthe Mbita assumed a significant role in the peace talks and the Cessation of Hostilities Agreement signed between extremist groups in December 2017.

She directly engaged in the discussions with the leaders of hostile groups. Marthe actively promotes the civil and political rights of women with local agencies and community leaders and unites international organizations and communities to work in cohesion.

Photo by Leila Thiam/Copyright © UN

"When I make someone feel at peace, when I help people live together peacefully, it enriches not only me but the country as a whole," expresses Marthe Mbita.

Daniela Soto, Indigenous Youth Leader, Colombia

(Photo by Deisy Tellez Giraldo/Copyright © UN)

Daniela Soto (22) is an indigenous woman belonging to the Nasa people. She is a philosophy student and a victim of armed conflict. She has been a coordinator for the youth program at the Regional Indigenous Council of Cauca (CRIC), where she has led training camps on the rights of indigenous peoples, youth, and women. She coordinated a Leadership camp for young women in Cauca for the construction and sustainability of peace... a pilot project of the UN Women Colombia.

"I come from a place that has historically been restive and violent for a long time. My people and I have suffered all kinds of violence based on racism, discrimination, and socio-economic differences. I wish that I can contribute to social upheaval. This is not just my responsibility, but the everyone's," says Daniela Soto emphatically.

Chapter 2

Section 1

UN and International Peace and Security

The United Nations faces enormous challenges even as it plays a pivotal role in maintaining international peace and security. How does the international body maintain world peace and security? The UN accomplishes this by working to prevent conflict, helping parties in conflict make peace, deploying peacekeepers, and creating the conditions to allow peace to hold and flourish. These activities often overlap and reinforce one another, to be effective.

The UN Security Council has the primary responsibility for international peace and security. The General Assembly and the Secretary-General play major, important, and complementary roles, along with other UN offices and bodies.

The UN predominantly uses the following to maintain world peace and security:

Preventive Diplomacy and Mediation: It is deemed as one of the most effective way to diminish human suffering and economic cost of conflicts. The UN plays an important role in conflict prevention, using diplomacy, good offices and mediation. Special envoys and political missions in the field are the important tool the Organization uses to bring peace. The Secretary-General of the United Nations has Special and Personal Representatives, Envoys and Advisers in many areas of the world.

Peacebuilding: United Nations peacebuilding activities are aimed at assisting countries emerging from conflict, reducing the risk of relapsing into conflict and laying the foundation for sustainable peace and development. The UN peacebuilding architecture comprises the Peacebuilding Commission, the Peacebuilding Fund and the Peacebuilding Support Office. The Peacebuilding Support Office assists and supports the Peacebuilding Commission with strategic advice and policy guidance, administers the Peacebuilding Fund and serves the Secretary-General in coordinating United Nations agencies in their peacebuilding efforts.

Peacekeeping: Peacekeeping has proven to be one of the most effective tools available to the UN to assist countries to navigate the difficult path from conflict to peace. Today's multidimensional peacekeeping operations are called upon not only to maintain peace and security, but also to facilitate political processes, protect civilians, assist in the disarmament, demobilization and reintegration of former combatants; support constitutional processes and the organization of elections, protect and promote human rights and assist in restoring the rule of law and extending legitimate state authority.

Peacekeeping operations get their mandates from the UN Security Council; their troops and police are contributed by Member States; and they are managed by the Department of Peace Operations and supported by the Department of Operational Support at UN Headquarters in New York.

There are 12 UN peacekeeping operations currently deployed and there have been a total of 71 deployed since 1948. In 2019, the Secretary-General launched the Action for Peacekeeping Initiative (A4P) to renew mutual political commitment to peacekeeping operations

Countering Terrorism

The United Nations is being increasingly called upon to coordinate the global fight against terrorism. Eighteen universal instruments against international terrorism have been elaborated within the framework of the United Nations system relating to specific terrorist activities. In September 2006, UN Member States adopted the United Nations Global Counter-Terrorism Strategy. This was the first time that Member States agreed to a common strategic and operational framework against terrorism.

Disarmament

The General Assembly and other bodies of the United Nations, supported by the Office for Disarmament Affairs, work to advance international peace and security through the pursuit of the elimination of nuclear weapons and other weapons of mass destruction and the regulation of conventional arms.

India's Contribution to UN Peacekeeping

India has an enduring and cherished history of service in the UN peacekeeping. She has contributed more troops than any other member nation. Till date, over 2,53,000 Indian soldiers have served in 49 of the 71 UN peacekeeping missions across the world since 1948. Currently, there are nearly 5,500 troops & police from India who have been deployed to UN peacekeeping missions, the fifth highest amongst troop-contributing countries (TCCs).

Beginning with participation in the UN operation in Korea in 1950s, India's mediation resolved the stalemate over prisoners of war in Korea and culminated in the signing of the armistice that ended the Korean War. India chaired the five-member **Neutral Nations Repatriation Commission** while the **Indian Custodian** Force oversaw the process of interviews and repatriation that followed.

The UN entrusted Indian armed forces with subsequent peace missions in the Middle East, Cyprus, and the Congo (since 1971, Zaire). India also served as chair of the three international commissions for supervision and control for Vietnam, Cambodia, and Laos established by the 1954 **Geneva Accords on Indochina.**

India has a distinguished tradition of sending women on UN peacekeeping missions. In 2007, India became the first country to deploy an all-women contingent to a UN peacekeeping mission. The **Formed Police Unit** in Liberia provided 24-hour guard duty and conducted night patrols in the capital Monrovia and helped to build the capability of the Liberian police. Hailed as role models, these female officers not only played a vital role in restoring security in the West African nation but also contributed to an increase in the number of women in the Liberia's security sector.

Additionally, the members of the female Indian Formed Police Unit also heralded themselves through humanitarian service, including organizing medical camps for Liberians, many of who had limited access to healthcare services.

Medical care is among the many services Indian peacekeepers provide to the communities in which they serve on behalf of the UNO. They also perform specialized tasks such as veterinary support and engineering services.

Indian troops join Danish and Swedish peacekeepers on a training exercise on a beach in Gaza in 1958 as part of the UN Emergency Force (UNEF).

Indian veterinarians serving with the **UN Mission in South Sudan (UNMISS),** ramped-up to help cattle herders who were losing much of their livestock to malnutrition and disease in the war- torn nation. The Indian contingent in South Sudan has gone the extra mile by providing vocational training and life-saving medical assistance, and carrying out significant road repair work.

The Indian contingent in the **Upper Nile region** includes the **Indian Battalion, and Horizontal Mechanical Engineering Company.** The Level two hospital, **Petroleum Platoon** and **Force Signal Unit** have all received UN medals of honour for their dedicated service in peacekeeping.

Indian peacekeepers have also fetched the ancient Indian practice of Yoga to UN missions. Members of the UN mission in Lebanon, United **Nations Interim Force in Lebanon (UNIFIL)** and UNMISS (South Sudan) celebrate International Yoga Day every year.

India has provided 17 **Force Commanders** in various missions. Besides them, India also had the distinction of providing two **Military Advisors,** one **Female Police Adviser** and one **Deputy Military Advisor** to the UN Secretary General

India was the first country to contribute to the **Trust Fund on Sexual Exploitation and Abuse,** that was established in 2016. India's enduring service has not come without   damage. As many as 173 Indian peacekeepers have paid the ultimate

India & The United Nations

price and have been martyred while serving with the United Nations. India has lost more peacekeepers than any other member state.

In September 2020, based on an urgent request received from the UN Secretariat, India deployed two medical teams of 15 medical personnel each at Goma (Democratic Republic of Congo) and Juba (South Sudan).

The hub of command-and-control center of MONUSCO (Mission de l'Organisation des Nations Unies pour la stabilisation en République démocratique du Congo) is located in Goma. The **Hospital by India** in Goma, operational since January 2005, has 90 Indian nationals including 18 specialists. With the rise in COVID-19 cases in the area, the "Level-3" facility, (highest level) of medical care provided by a deployed UN unit, is now being upgraded to a Level-3 Plus facility. The "Level-2 plus" Hospital by India in Juba, South Sudan (UNMISS), operational since December 2016, has 77 Indian nationals including 12 specialists. The Indian facility in Juba is presently the one of highest level of medical facilities existing in South Sudan. This facility is now being upgraded from Level-2 plus to a Level-3 facility.

Section 2

Role of business 'actors' in peacebuilding

The approach to peace building has significantly transformed in the last 30-odd years. The vision of a group of people sitting around a table for peace talks is increasingly paving the way to a more expansive, inclusive, and representative schemes of the best way to end armed conflict and achieve lasting stability. The purpose behind this change is simple: Those affected by armed conflict should have a say in ending and recovering from it through reconciliation and post-war rehabilitation of affected economies.

What peacebuilding role can local business play? Who can partner with businesses in the interest of peace? – these are the questions being raised. Most conflicts are, at least partly, driven by economic agendas. Local business practices can be significant factors in generating unrest and violence. These include corruption, rent seeking on a massive scale and a weakening of democracy. They also include neglect of more labour-intensive industries, a worsening of inequality and a deepening of poverty.

While some local businesses benefit from bullets and bandages, for most, war is devastating for business. This can be the fundamental motivation for business involvement in peacebuilding. Moreover, their lack of a uniform agenda and their varied interests provide opportunities and challenges in identifying their potential to help build peace.

The following initiatives would help clarify the role local businesses can play in peacebuilding and begin to build a legitimate private sector peace initiative:

- Publicising the costs of conflict to business leaders would help them recognising the economic cost of war and strife. Organising collective business action would help businesses use their political contacts towards peaceful outcomes.

- Developing a positively perceived private sector will help redress the perception that all local businesses have a history of collusion and exert strong a political influence.

- Business leaders can be influenced to become individual champions for peace and provide critical leadership in a peace process.

- National-level business can direct its knowledge of corporate governance and experience with social investment and policy dialogue to the interests of peacebuilding.

- The experience of provincial/regional businesses and grassroots/informal traders operating enterprises during violent conflict can reform the peace process.

- Businesses have readymade networks in the form of chambers of commerce and business associations. The international community can be both a partner and supporter of businesses that, in turn, support peace.

To engineer the shift of businesses towards engagement in peacebuilding, the following combination of activities is needed:

- Awareness raising, not only among the private sector itself, but among other local and international peacebuilding organizations
- Further research to identify the different types of roles according to the size and nature of the business community, as well as the type and stage of conflict
- Increased implementation of practical businesses-for-peace initiatives that are supported and promoted by the international community.

Women, youth, and civil society are progressively taking part in peace and security conversations. Still largely underexplored, however, is the role of businesspeople.

Josie Lianna Kaye, Director of TrustWorks Global, specializes in peace mediation, peacebuilding, and violence prevention, with a particular focus on including business actors in peace and advising companies on conflict-sensitivity in complex contexts.

Kaye mentioned two important facets to this question of role of business in peacebuilding. First is what we understand by 'business actors.' In fragile states, most of the international community's attention focuses on extractive actors associated with the so-called 'resource curse'.

Mainly due to the large global footprint of such actors in contexts where land and natural resources like oil, are highly contested, the impacts are more likely to be disruptive and palpable if not effectively managed by all stakeholders.

When we broaden our definition of business actors to include formal/informal and local/international actors, it is evident that the state and local populace depend on business for taxes, financing, and services/livelihoods. Focusing only on the negative impacts of extractive industries is therefore extremely reductive.

The second important aspect to consider is perspective: Many business actors may be providing jobs to vulnerable employees, and simultaneously financing the warring parties, directly or indirectly.

Other business actors may be engaged in levels of corruption that are undermining state governance and the social contract, while actively seeking to mediate an end to violence or a minimum level of stability and predictability for their activities.

Others may seek to foster the dynamics of reconciliation in the workplace while inadvertently contributing to violence through their value and supply chains.

The extractive industries may have positive impacts —providing jobs, energy, infrastructure, and other social benefits. So the answer to the question of what role businesses can play in peace restoration, is that in any given context, the response is never binary and there are always a multitude of business actors that have both negative and positive impacts. To fully grasp what these are one needs to suspend binary thinking, i.e. legit businesses are 'good' and illicit businesses are 'bad'.

There are several excellent examples. There is the famous example of Roland 'Tiny' Rowland — the former CEO of the Lonrho conglomerate, an extractives multinational corporation—who played a critical role as a mediator and facilitator in Mozambique in the 1980s.

There was the 'Consultative Business Movement' that supported the negotiation of a new political settlement in post-apartheid South Africa.

In Northern Ireland, the business community actively lobbied for peace and organized meetings with all the political parties that participated in the peace talks.

And more recently, in Yemen, representatives of some of the most important business families actively worked behind the scenes to seek a peaceful end to the conflict at various points from 2011.

In many of the above contexts, the predominant form of engagement was with formal, legit business actors but there are also many examples of engagement with illegal actors, particularly behind the scenes and on the fringes.

A good example of this is the Anéfis process in Mali in 2015, which contributed to reducing violence between armed groups and communities related to competition over trafficking and trade routes.

In most strife contexts, however, the lines between legit and illicit can become quickly quite 'fuzzy', since they use the same roads, services, and infrastructures and because war economies cannot be neatly 'partitioned' off from the rest of the economy.

What is intriguing about these examples is that they predominantly pertain to cases where business actors themselves sought to be actively involved in formal peace processes.

How can business actors contribute to peace?

Business actors can be engaged in diverse ways. It would be a fallacy to limit their role to one of mediator or 'peace lobbyist', particularly since not all business actors want to play this role.

It is much more important for peacemakers to incorporate the positive and negative roles of business actors (because of their core operations, and their supply and value chains) into the elaboration of peace-related strategies.

Business actors form a vital part of any democratic society, so they should be included on strategic grounds because we know that the more inclusive the peace process, the more sustainable it is likely to be.

As a result of their horizontal and vertical linkages, business actors have significant political and societal influence that can be brought to bear on the mediation process.

From a substantive perspective, business actors have specific knowledge about formal and informal centers of power, the economy, trade routes, supply chains, conditions on the ground, intimate knowledge of how the country is integrated in regional and global political economies.

All of this can help inform the peace mediation strategy and, potentially, the provisions of a peace settlement. For example, in Yemen, while the private sector was only given three seats (out of 565), during the **National Dialogue Conference,** the business community worked actively behind the scenes to try to ensure that economic issues were adequately and comprehensively addressed during that process.

From an implementation perspective, businesses with their vast networks, can leverage their political capital and knowledge in a manner that can help advocate for the implementation of the agreement in the post-conflict phases, and support such implementation more directly.

As with the reintegration of ex-**Fuerzas Armadas Revolucionarias de Colombia (FARC)** combatants in Colombia, for example, illicit business actors particularly are likely to have a vast wealth of knowledge about conflict dynamics.

Many communities may be dependent on them for survival, and the failure to bring them on board of any emerging peace settlement and to consider alternative livelihood strategies could result in them deliberately or inadvertently undermining the peace process.

Unlike dialogues with civil society, women, youth, and non-state armed groups and even terrorist groups, which are more 'codified' in **UN Security** Council resolutions, protocols, trainings, guidance notes, practice and mind-sets, engagement with business actors is dependent on the individual initiative of the mediator or mediation team.

There are **no** UN resolutions, protocols, or guidance on how to include business actors in peace. If we use peace agreements as a proxy for understanding the extent of inclusion of business actors, research demonstrates that only 2.5 per cent of peace agreements signed since 1990 reference both legit and illegal business actors and such references tend to be superficial in nature. This is a major blind-spot.

As such, despite the conflict-reducing and peace-promoting potential of business actors, such opportunities are being consistently missed, undermining prospects for peace. And when mediators do try to include them, it too often comes as an afterthought to try to get them to finance the post-conflict recovery/peacebuilding phase.

Current Challenges

These challenges are compounded by several factors. First, business actors tend to be perceived only as economic actors, despite their political interests, motivations, and effects.

Second, too often it is assumed that business actors are not interested in peace and are interested only in profit, despite the diversity of business actors and interests which need to be contextualized, understood, and leveraged.

Third, business actors tend to be viewed primarily through the 'jobs' lens, and only once a peace agreement has been signed. Business actors can contribute much more than jobs and including them further 'upstream' in the peace agreement would be much more effective.

Lastly, business actors are not seen as natural partners for the UN. There is a certain cultural 'discomfort' with engaging with profit-seeking entities despite the increasingly strong awareness of the contributions business actors can make to peace.

The work of TrustWorks Global in this domain suggests that policy changes are required both amongst member states, including within the UN Security Council, and the UN Secretariat to ensure a 'business lens' is applied to all peace-related endeavors.

A key step in this regard could be a UN Security Council resolution on the role of business actors in peace, which would not only clarify this role but also give a mandate to UN teams to engage with business.

The predicaments mentioned above can be overcome by expanding the discourse and practice of inclusion to business actors — formal/informal, legit/illicit, local/international. In practice, this means ensuring business actors are more consistently included in country/mediation analyses, peace mediation strategies, and in formal and informal dialogue processes across all tracks.

A 'business lens' and not just an 'employment lens' can assist in ensuring not only direct engagement with business actors whenever possible. Also ensuring that all strategies -humanitarian, development and in peacebuilding -are sensitive and well-adapted to the positive and negative roles that business actors play is needed.

Since research and best practices on engagement of business actors are relatively sketchy, compared to engagement with other actors, additional efforts to expand the UN's knowledge concerning successful strategies and risk/opportunity management would also be useful.

Lastly, it is helpful to recognize that including business actors in peace does not require 'reinventing the wheel'. Many of the strategies for engaging women, youth, and civil society on the one hand, and for engaging with non-state armed or terrorist groups on the other hand, can be adapted and applied to business actors, while taking into consideration the specific risks and opportunities that engagement with them in any given context may pose.

It is widely accepted that the private sector has a primary responsibility in building economic and social well-being. There is also an emerging understanding about the need to bring the business as one of the actors to the same table where we discuss conflict prevention, post-conflict peacebuilding and recovery in fragile, conflict-prone societies.

The UN and the world need partnerships and multi-stakeholder approaches between governments, civil society institutions and corporations. It is worth noting that the **Organisation for Economic Co-operation and Development (OECD)** development ministers in 2001 encouraged trends towards partnership with business - domestic and international - to raise awareness of how firms can be good corporate citizens, avoid feeding the negative dynamics of conflict, and make positive economic and social contributions to preventing violence.

In the spirit of corporate citizenship and civic mindedness, the private sector itself must assume a responsibility, also in uncertain conditions, to help prevent and mitigate conflict.

The actions of private companies during conflicts - and the corporate ethics behind those actions - and sensitivity to human rights are important in this regard.

Conflict today is too often caused by the struggle to exploit natural resources. The private sector's contributions towards instability and conflict if it provides a source of finance to armed groups in exchange for natural wealth (diamonds, gold, timber, etc.).

In this regard, Security Council Resolution 1306 of 2000 banning uncertified rough diamond imports from Sierra Leone, was a major step in recognizing the role of the private sector in conflicts.

It should also be noted that some industries have engaged in self-regulation with various degree of success peacebuilding requires a huge economic investment and the involvement of investors. The key challenge is to rebuild economies in such a way that the benefits of recovery are spread as widely as possible across society.

In recent years the **Economic and Social Council** has taken a more active role in developing a capacity to respond to the countries emerging from conflict and thus helping to prevent human conditions from worsening.

The Council continues to address the roots of conflict throughout its work. This year the Council will concentrate on the least developed countries at its substantive session.

In the preparations the UN has also focused on those countries that are emerging from conflict. In the light of their experiences, the private sector is essential as a development partner - with the support of the international community in backing the recovery efforts when necessary.

Economic and Social Council (ECOSOC) and the Security Council have begun to collaborate in these endeavors. However much more can be done by the ***General Assembly, the Security Council and ECOSOC*** working together to develop a comprehensive and a more rapid-response capacity for countries in special situations, where speed, scale and time are of the essence.

The UN must also develop a sufficiently long-term perspective towards both sustainable development and conflict prevention. The High-level Panel on Threats, Challenges and Change will help the Organization undertake reform measures that will make it more agile and more flexible in responding to the challenges of the 21st century. The Security Council and the Economic and Social Council stand ready to play their part in contributing to strengthening the United Nations in this strategic area.

The Diplomatic Council of the UN

The Diplomatic Council is a unique organisation with consultative status to the United Nations. The Council is the meeting point of a global think tank, a global business network and a charitable organisation. The primary objective of the Diplomatic Council is to resolve the biggest challenges mankind is currently facing – environmental crisis, poverty, terrorism and inequality to name a few. It links diplomacy, businesses, science and technology and society's frontrunners to break down the barriers to lasting peace.

The Diplomatic Council enjoys special consultative status with the UN. It has been granted by the United Nations the highest status that can be achieved for a non-governmental organisation (NGO): the special consultative status with the **Economic and Social Council (ECOSOC)** of the United Nations. This status entitles the Diplomatic Council to attend UN sessions and make written and oral statements at international UN conferences and events.

It will consequently have the opportunity to globally support the interest of economic diplomacy, express its views and influence the work of the **Economic and Social Council:** a flourishing economy that brings prosperity to mankind is one of the best peace guarantors worldwide.

Diplomatic Council members can apply to become Diplomatic Council UN delegates and attend UN sessions in New York, Geneva, and Vienna. By offering this unique opportunity, the Diplomatic Council opens to its members access to one of the most exclusive, global contact networks with regard to economic and social issues.

DIPLOMATIC COUNCIL ACCREDITED ACCORDING TO ARTICLE 71 OF THE UN CHARTER

According to Article 71 of the UN Charter, the **Economic and Social Council (ECOSOC)** of the United Nations has enclosed the **Diplomatic Council** in its circle of accredited non-governmental organisations. In consequence, the Diplomatic Council is granted consultative status with the ECOSOC. The consultative relationship is governed by the ECOSOC resolution 1996/31, which outlines the eligibility requirements for consultative status, rights, and obligations of NGOs in consultative status.

Moreover, this consultative status is the highest status a non-governmental organization can obtain with the United Nations. The nomination of the **Diplomatic Council was made by 14 African States, 11 Asian States, six Eastern European States, 10 Latin American and Caribbean States and 13 Western European and other States.**

The main requirements to gain eligibility for consultative status with ECOSOC include:

- the work of the NGO must be relevant to the work of ECOSOC;
- the NGO must have a transparent structure based on a legal constitution;
- it must have an established headquarters with an executive officer;
- it must provide to the Committee financial statements;
- it should have a representative structure such as the Diplomatic Council has with its Chairs, Vice-Chairs, Directors, Permanent Representatives, Representatives and Delegates.

The work of the ECOSOC is conducted through several sessions and preparatory meetings, roundtable and panel discussions. Once a year, the Diplomatic Council is invited to attend the four-week session of the ECOSOC alternating between New York and Geneva with the opportunity to collaborate in the work of the United Nations by making oral and written statements and expressing its views.

In this connection, the diplomatic actions of the Diplomatic Council are executed by the **Council of Ambassadors** while the business activities are driven by the **Diplomatic Council Chairmen or Chairwomen, Vice Chairs and Directors.** The nomination of Diplomatic Council UN delegates is organized by the **Secretariat General.**

The Diplomatic Council is invited to attend all conferences and other events of the Economic and Social Council and make written and oral statements at these events. It is also encouraged to participate in debates, interactive dialogues, panel discussions and informal meetings and has the option of organizing its own side events at the New York, Geneva, and Vienna headquarters.

The highest Diplomatic Council representatives are entitled to receive the "United Nations Annual Ground Pass" which allows them access to the UN headquarters in New York, Geneva and Vienna for the duration of one year.

The ECOSOC grants consultative status for the purpose of securing expert information or advice from Diplomatic Council members around the world.

Members of the Diplomatic Council take actions on important topics concerning the future of mankind. It can participate in the Commission on Sustainable Development, the Commission on the Status of Women, the Commission for Social Development, the Commission on Population and Development, the Commission on Crime Prevention and Criminal Justice, the Commission on Narcotic Drugs, the Commission on Science and Technology for Development, the Statistical Commission and the Forum on Forests as well as the permanent Forum for Flora and Fauna.

In addition to the involvement in the ECOSOC commissions, the United Nations considers the Diplomatic Council a multiplier to spread the positions of the United Nations all over the world. By granting the consultative status, the UN expects the Diplomatic Council to execute the following tasks:

- provide expert analysis on issues from its experience
- serve as an early warning agent
- help monitor and implement international agreements
- help raise public awareness of relevant issues
- play a major role in advancing UN goals and objectives
- contribute with essential information at organization events.

Through the ECOSOC accreditation, the Diplomatic Council is invited to attend the session of the **Human Rights Council (HRC)** and make written and oral statements. This includes participation at the **Universal Periodic Reviews (UPR)** which involves a review of the human rights records of all 192 United Nations Member States once every four years.

The **Diplomatic Council UN master plan 2030** provides that the Diplomatic Council gradually execute the tasks related to the consultative status.

The objective of the Diplomatic Council is to be represented by at least one delegate at all relevant events of the Economic and Social Council.

Chapter 3

Section 1

The Sustainable Development Goals (SDGs)

"Just as our vision behind Agenda 2030 is lofty, our goals are comprehesive. It gives priority to the problems that have endured through the past decades. And, it reflects our evolving understanding of the social, economic and environmental linkages that define our lives...The sustainable development of one-sixth of humanity will be of great consequence to the world and our beautiful planet."

--Narendra Modi, Prime Minister of India

The international community, through the United Nations, has set in motion a historic plan – 17 Sustainable Development Goals – that aims to build a more prosperous, more equal, and more secure world by the year 2030.

The 17 SDGs and 169 targets are part of the 2030 Agenda for Sustainable Development adopted by 193 Member States at the UN General Assembly Summit in September 2015, and which came into effect on 1 January 2016. These goals are the result of an unprecedented consultative process that brought national governments and millions of citizens from across the globe together to negotiate and adopt the global path to sustainable development for the next 15 years.

The SDGs and targets will stimulate action in the following critically important areas: poverty, hunger, education, health and well-being, education, gender equality, water and sanitation, energy, economic growth and decent work, infrastructure, industry and innovation, reducing inequalities, sustainable cities, consumption and production, climate action, ecosystems, peace and justice, and partnership. This comprehensive agenda recognises that it is no longer sufficient just to focus on economic growth, but on fairer and more equal societies, and a safer and more prosperous planet. It recognises that the tasks of peace, justice, environmental protection, and industrial development are not disconnected from each other, but part of the same change. It recognises, above all, that global and interconnected challenges can only be fought with global and interconnected solutions. It is an ambitious plan that will require a renewed global partnership between governments, businesses, the civil society, and individuals. As we make progress towards achieving the 169 targets, we will reorient national and global development on a more sustainable, more resilient path.

The SDGs and targets will stimulate action in the following critically important areas: poverty, hunger, education, health and well-being, education, gender equality, water and sanitation, energy, economic growth and decent work, infrastructure, industry and innovation, reducing inequalities, sustainable cities, consumption and production, climate action, ecosystems, peace and justice, and partnership. This comprehensive agenda recognises that it is no longer sufficient just to focus on economic growth, but on fairer and more equal societies, and a safer and more prosperous planet. It recognises that the tasks of peace, justice, environmental protection, and industrial development are not disconnected from each other, but part of the same change. It recognises, above all, that global and interconnected challenges can only be fought with global and interconnected solutions. It is an ambitious plan that will require a renewed global partnership between governments, businesses, the civil society, and individuals. As we make progress towards achieving the 169 targets, we will reorient national and global development on a more sustainable, more resilient path.

Leave No One Behind

At the core of this global agenda for 2030 is the principle of universality: 'Leave No One Behind'. It is critical to the implementation of these targets that they should be relevant to all governments and actors. Development in all its dimensions must be inclusive of all people, everywhere, and should be built through the participation of everyone, especially the most vulnerable and marginalised.

India's Leading Role

The Government of India is strongly committed to the 2030 Agenda, including the SDGs, as evidenced by the statements of the Prime Minister and other senior Ministers at national and international meetings. India's national development goals and its "sab ka saath, sab ka vikas" or "development with all, and for all," policy initiatives for inclusive development converge well with the SDGs, and India will play a leading role in determining the success of the SDGs, globally. As Prime Minister Narendra Modi noted, "These goals reflect our evolving understanding of the social, economic and environmental linkages that define our lives.".

National Action on the SDGs in India

NITI Aayog, the Government of India's premier think tank, has been entrusted with the task of coordinating the SDGs. NITI Aayog has undertaken a mapping of schemes as they relate to the SDGs and their targets, and has identified lead and supporting ministries for each target. They have adopted a government-wide approach to sustainable development, emphasising the interconnected nature of the SDGs across economic, social and environmental pillars. States have been advised to undertake a similar mapping of their schemes, including centrally sponsored schemes.

In addition, the Ministry of Statistics and Programme Implementation (MoSPI) has been leading discussions for developing national indicators for the SDGs. State governments are key to India's progress on the SDG Agenda and several of them have already initiated action on implementing the SDGs.

State Governments are a crucial driving force for SDG progress

State governments are key to India's progress on the SDG Agenda as they are best placed to 'put people first' and to ensuring that 'no one is left behind'. Many of the Government's flagship programmes such as Swachh Bharat, Make in India, Skill India, and Digital India are at the core of the SDGs. State and local governments play a pivotal role in many of these programmes.

The role of local governments is equally important; 15 of the 17 SDGs directly relate to activities undertaken by local governments in the country. State governments are paying keen attention to visioning, planning, budgeting, and developing implementation and monitoring systems for the SDGs.

UN Support for Localising the SDGs

Supporting the consultative process, post-2015

Advocating the broad-based consultative process that characterises the new global agenda process, the United Nations in India supported the participation of civil society organisations, think tanks and the Indian media in discussions at intergovernmental negotiations, seminars on financing for development and sustainable development and side sessions at the International Conference on Financing for Development at Addis Ababa and during the General Assembly in New York.

Strategic support to address the interconnectedness of issues

The UN Country Team in India supports NITI Aayog in its efforts to address the interconnectedness of the goals, to ensure that no one is left behind and to advocate for adequate financing to achieve the SDGs. In close collaboration with NITI Aayog and partners, the UN has supported thematic consultations on the SDGs to bring together various state governments, central ministries, civil society organisations and academia to deliberate on specific SDGs.

Support to State Governments

The UN in India currently supports state governments in localising the SDGs to address key development challenges at the state level.

MEFCC's mantra: Combining Sustainable Development with Environmental Protection

Over the last seven years, under Prime Minister Narendra Modi, India has taken giant steps towards sustainable development, digitisation, self-reliance and financial inclusion. Schemes such as Atmanirbhar Bharat and Make in India have given impetus to social entrepreneurship and environmental protection.

Environmental protection and ecological balance have taken centre-stage so much so that the Ministry of Environment and Forests has now been renamed as the Ministry of Environment, Forests and Climate Change.

The Pradhan Mantri Rozgar Yojana, and voluntary relinquishment of LPG subsidy by millions of Indians has touched the lives of millions of others across the nation by providing clean fuel. Ease of doing business and schemes like Mudra to encourage setting up of micro- and women-led businesses have mitigated the nagging issue of unemployment in the country.

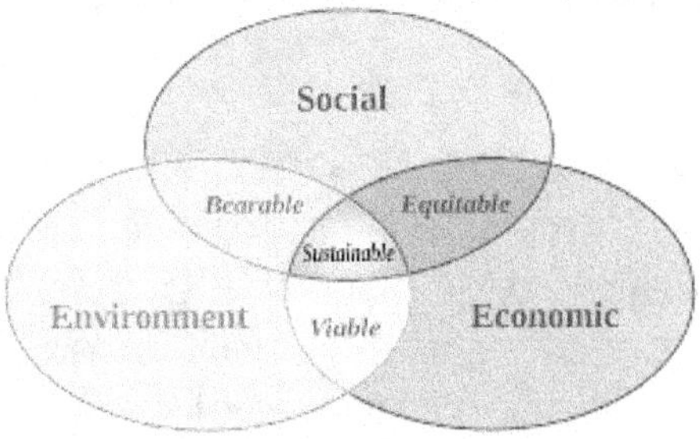

Source: The Internet

The Modi government's objectives when it came to power, of ensuring inclusive all-round national development, sabka saath, sabka vikaas, have seen fruition of many while a few others remain.

The country has taken giant leaps to curtail the rearing threat of terrorism and efforts have been made to improve the quality of life in regions torn by sectarian violence for decades. As a result, socio-economic growth indicators are turning green. Foreign relations with neighboring countries (in the SAARC region) and world powers like the USA and the Russian Federation have improved. India is now counted among economic superpowers of the world.

The highly aspirational district programs and 'Gram Swaraj Abhiyan' have been launched by the Government of India (GOI) mainly for the backward districts of the country. Government interventions under these two programs have produced tangible results in terms of eradicating unemployment and ensuring 'Panchayat Raj' (self-governance) at the grassroots level.

Schemes like 'Poshan', 'Indradhanush', 'Saubhagya', 'Ujala', 'Ujjwala', 'Pradhan Mantri Jan Dhan Yojana', 'Pradhan Mantri Suraksha Bima Yojana', 'Pradhan Mantri Jeevan Jyoti Bima Yojana' have been designed and implemented to ensure inclusive development.

Picture Courtesy: International Institute for Sustainable Development

"Sabka Saath, Sabka Vikas" (Inclusive Development, Together) is GOI's development mantra. The high-impact schemes are carefully planned and designed to target development at the grassroots -- to enrich the district ecosystems. The schemes empower local governments to improve services of critical sectors such as education and healthcare. They have created new avenues for self-employment,

India & The United Nations

agri-marketing, and sustainable livelihood for people in villages, empowering citizens to chart their own growth stories.

Digitisation and proliferation of telecommunications has connected the remote parts of India to the rest of the world. Developments in science and technology are no more the exclusive prerogative of the urban populace as the youth in villages too can access them. Technology has levelled the field for all surmounting all barriers -- of geography, language and devices.

The Ministry of Environment, Forest & Climate Change (MEFCC), hitherto a predominantly regulatory and governing body, is now viewed as a 'facilitator'. The ministry's objective is to ensure norms against deforestation, environmental pollution, and poaching are enforced with more teeth. MEFCC's goal is to ensure sustainable development combined with environment protection.

The key challenges faced by MEFCC of the Modi cabinet were:

1. Creating 'Ease of Doing Business' by ushering transparency and speed in green clearances

2. Pollution reduction (air/water/soil/noise)

3. Increase in forest and mangrove cover

4. Successful and efficient wildlife conservation management

5. Sustainable Development linked indelibly with environmental conservation

6. Creating avenues for eco-friendly employment generation

7. Use of technology in environmental management

8. Image management at international fora – to be able to better negotiate agreements in India's interest

9. Building and strengthening public connect with government and creating awareness of schemes and their benefits

10.

shutterstock.com · 1955306350

The environmental norms have seen restructuring and digitisation has enabled a well-oiled system to grant clearances. As a result, time taken to obtain clearances has reduced from 600 days to no more than 160 days. The clearance system has witnessed unprecedented technological advancements to become 'participatory'. This is the hallmark of governance by the current government in India.

Streamlining clearance processes was a major challenge before the GOI. The Environmental Clearance, Coastal Regulation Zone (CRZ) Clearance and the Forest Clearance processes are now possible to obtain online. The clerance procedures, which earlier stalled development projects, including projects of national significance and strategic homeland security, are now transparent, quick and efficient.

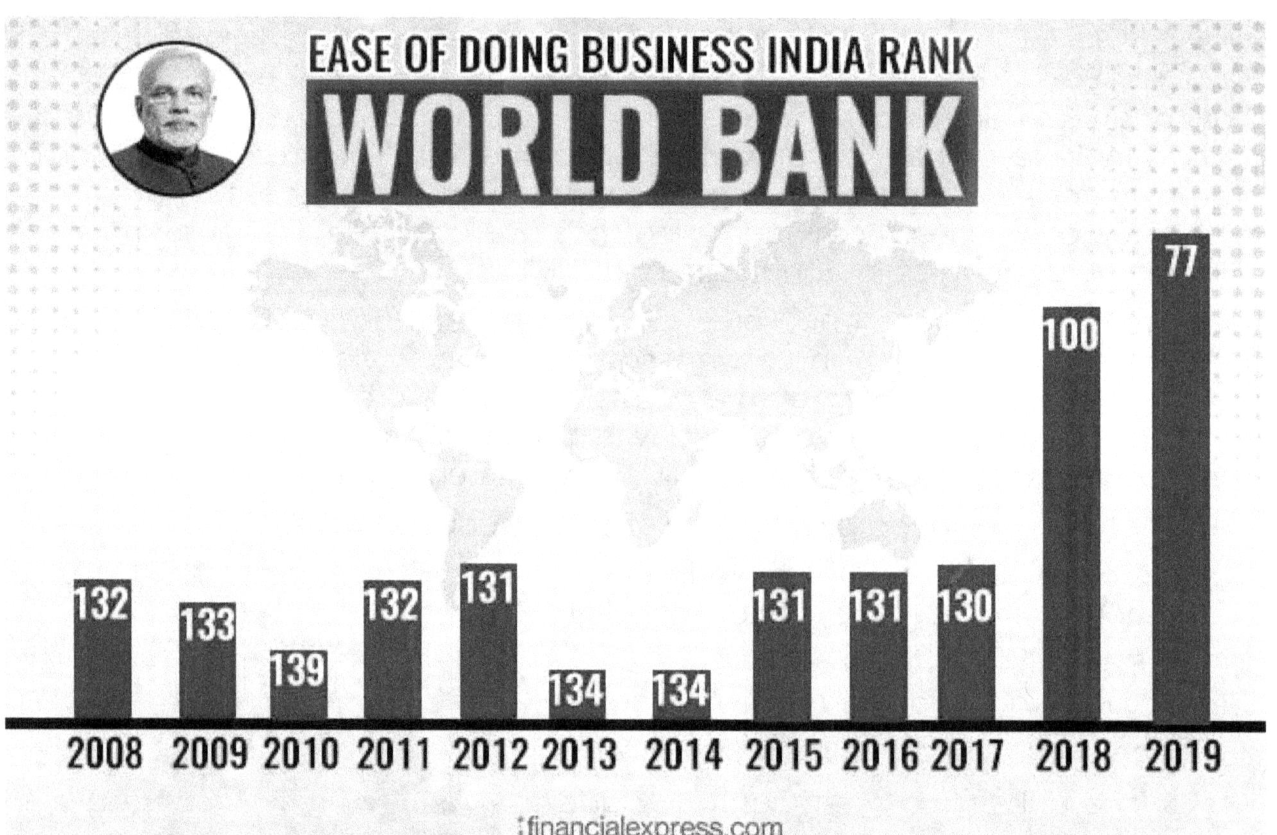

Picture Courtesy: The Financial Express

Decentralization of power by permitting district authorities, state pollution control boards, and regional offices of the ministry to grant project clearances, has ushered in speed and accountability into the system. Now, MEFCC leads the way for other ministries in clearance processes that are fast and ensure 'ease of doing business'.

In total commitment to safer and cleaner rivers, India has stepped up online monitoring of pollution by industries. A relentless 24/7 emission/effluent checking system has been established in over 2,300 industries in 17 categories. Over 700 industries have been brought under online monitoring of industrial pollution to clean the River Ganga. Management of industrial pollution has now been simplified. The worrying menace of black liquor discharge and spent wash into the Ganga is brought under control. Pollution of the Ganga has witnessed a significant downturn from 131 tons per day to 67 tons per day.

India has emerged as a key player in environmental negotiations in the world and PM Modi played a prominent role in the Paris Agreement on climate change and the establishment of the International Solar Alliance to combat climate change. India has positioned itself as an 'environmentally responsible' nation and is the global host for the 'World Environment Day'.

India has been particularly recognized as a front runner in environmental protection and climate change interventions. By ushering in a new era with the introduction of electric cars and scooters, India is playing a major role in phasing out ozone-depleting poisonous emissions.

India & The United Nations

Our bit done for the protection of our only home- Mother Earth, has come for praise by peer countries. India has been the recipient of accolades like the award presented to late Anil Madhav Dave, Minister of State, for his leadership in the Kigali Amendment to the Montreal Protocol.

Among other changes made to achieve sustainable development goals are better management of Coastal Regulation Zone (CRZ). It has been made transparent and freed from ambiguity. The High Tide Line, Low Tide Line, Hazard Line, and Eco-Sensitive Areas have been mapped out to remove subjectivity and bureaucratic hassles. Coastal management has undergone a 'sea-change' (pun intended!). It has been transformed without affecting the aquatic eco-systems while positively impacting the socio-economics of coastal communities.

The introduction of the National Air Quality Index (NAQI) has effected a paradigm shift to air pollution control in India. Protection of air quality has seen nation-wide participation from aware citizens and the fight is not confined to a few environmentalists. Green Good Deeds has turned into a mass movement in the country.

A case in point is the improved air quality in Delhi in the years 2017-2018 as compared to 2016 by adopting a scientific 42-point graded action plan for air pollution control. The National Clean Air Plan for enhancing the air quality was implemented at a cost of Rs 650 Crore.

MEFCC has amended the six cardinal pollution control rules intended to achieve total waste management. For over a decade now domestic solid waste has been collected at the doorstep by the city municipal corporations and segregated (into wet and dry) at source (the household level).

Waste segregation at source is being adopted with gusto by the country's urban populace. The reason for this phenomenal change is the robust campaign launched under the 'Swachch Bharat' initiative by the Modi government.

Committees have been constituted to oversee the implementation of the six pollution control laws in different states and the state governments have been sensitized to its provisions and need for timely implementation.

Winds of change

The Indian Forest Act, 1927, has been amended to omit bamboo from the definition of 'trees' with the intent of encouraging farmers to grow bamboo outside forests and increase their income. Bamboo-based industries have received an impetus through this move. And stories of farmers making crores of rupees have hogged the headlines in the media.

A simple step has revitalized the bamboo-based industry and bettered the lives of bamboo-farmers and traders. This small amendment has banished the 'inspector-raj' that plagued the bamboo industry so far.

Thanks to the MEFCC, 27 states and union territories have now exempted bamboo, which is a commonly grown agro-forestry species, from felling and transit permits. Farmers and those who wish to harvest and transport bamboo grown on their private (non-forest) land no longer need to obtain permissions, or an authority letter from the Forest Department. They have been freed from the legal and regulatory bondages faced in the cultivation of bamboo in their agricultural fields and other private areas.

Picture Courtesy: downtoearth.org.in (Bamboo grove)

About 20 million people are involved in bamboo-related activities in India. One ton of bamboo provides 350 man-days of employment. An empowering regulatory ecosystem for bamboo cultivation will increase employment in the country. It is GoI's vision to boost the quality of life of bamboo-dependent communities, artisans, forest dwellers and other marginalized sections of the society.

As the Forest Survey of India (FSI, Dehradun) reports, there has been a sizable increase in forest cover over the last four years. An increase of 7,843 km2 of forest and tree cover is recorded as per the FSI report, 2017 (year-on-year increase from 2015).

Forest and green cover in the country has reached 24.39 per cent of its geographic area. Area under forest and mangroves has increased, despite multiple challenges such as unauthorized deforestation and expansion of human settlements into the country's lung spaces and wildlife habitats. The desired outcome here is that this development has brought the ministry out of a state of policy paralysis.

Large corpuses collected as net present value (NPV) as part of the forest diversion cases lay idle in banks with no expenditure avenues. The Modi government has enacted Compensatory Afforestation Fund Act, 2016, (CAMPA Act) and issued the draft CAMPA Rules. States have been empowered to use the funds for forestry activities paving the way for rapid increase in India'sforest cover.

India & The United Nations

Picture Courtesy: Press Information Bureau (GOI)

The GoI has intensified its focus on wildlife conservation with a Comprehensive National Wildlife Action Plan 2017-2031 set in motion. The budgetary allocation under the Central share of "Centrally Sponsored Scheme – Integrated Development of Wildlife Habitat (IDWH)", which was Rs. 66.78 crore during the FY 2013-14, has been increased by a whopping 147 percent to Rs. 165.00 crore for the FY 2018-19.

Particular attention is given to streamlining the regulatory mechanism which has been bolstered to mitigate human-wildlife conflicts. The ex-gratia compensation rate for human deaths in wildlife conflict has been increased from Rs 2 lakh to Rs 5 lakh per person. This signifies an increase of 150 per cent. As mentioned earlier, India's effective intervention measures to reduce man-animal conflict has attracted international attention and appreciation.

Eco-Sensitive Zones (ESZ) are being carved out by GOI around 'Protected Areas' (PA) like national parks and wildlife sanctuaries to serve as buffer regions to balance local economic growth and conservation imperatives. As of March 2018, ESZs for 459 PAs have been notified as 'Draft/Final'. During the period 2004-2014, only 24 Draft and 8 Final ESZ notifications were published. However, in the past four years (2014-2018), 299 Draft and 154 Final notifications have been issued by adopting scientific approaches.

Following ESZ finalization, wildlife conservation and landscape planning have been stepped up. A more aggressive, but scientific approach, has been adopted by eliminating uncertainties and ambiguities. The hassles of resettlement and rehabilitation of local people in the absence of final ESZ boundaries have been obliterated. This has vitalized the process of "Ease of Doing Business" outside the notified ESZ boundaries while guaranteeing sufficient scientific conservation measures within the protected areas.

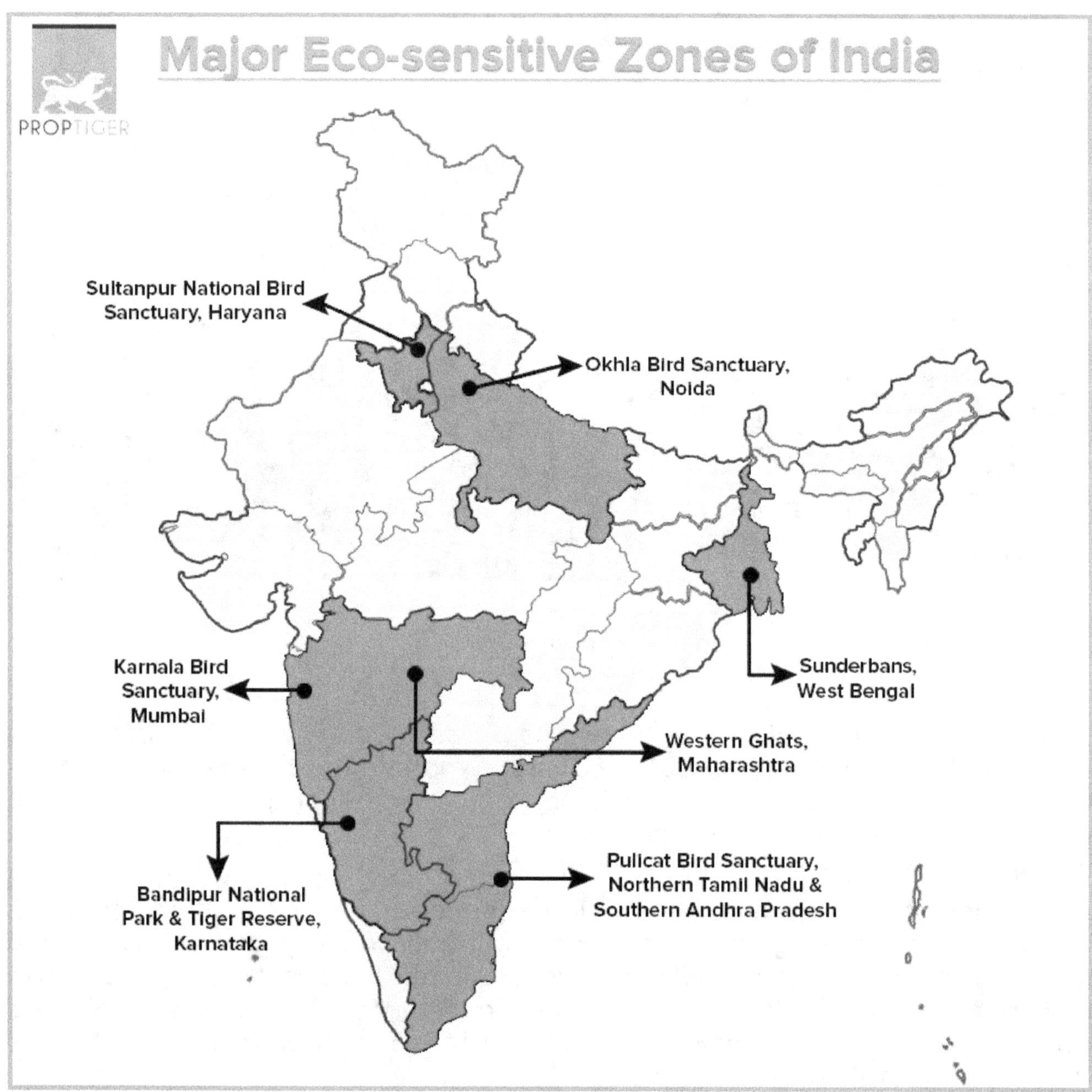

Source: pinterest.com

The breaking news as of September 21, 2021, is that India (PM Modi) will raise the issues related to climate change at the UN General Assembly (UNGA) meeting scheduled during the month along with curbing terrorism in the country and India's strained relations with China. US President Joe Biden has welcomed this move by India to set into motion dialogues between the two nations on the above pertinent issues, especially climate change.

MEFCC's image today has been transformed into a more visionary and facilitative body rather than just a regulator. This has been hailed as 'progressive' by governments across the world. The ministry has shown that environmental protection is not just a regulatory issue but a means to achieve sustainable development and employment generation.

MEFCC's comprehensive "Green Skill Development Program" (GSDP) was launched in association with the 70 Environmental Information Systems (ENVIS) centres and the National Skill Development Mission.

Over 30 skill-development programs were conducted during 2018-19, covering diverse topics like pollution monitoring (air/water/soil), setting up and operative issues of sewage treatment plants (STPs), effluent treatment plant (ETPs) and common effluent treatment plant (CETPs).

Courses in solid waste and forest management, water budgeting and auditing, conservation of river dolphins, wildlife management, and para taxonomy (including People's Biodiversity Registers or PBRs), mangroves conservation, bamboo management and livelihood generation were taught in nearly 70 institutes countrywide.

Picture Courtesy:

Press Information Bureau (GOI)

A whopping 5.6 lakh Indians are expected to be skilled by 2020-21 under the GSDP. They can be employed either directly or indirectly in industries, non-governmental organizations (NGOs), academic institutions, government agencies, and quasi-governmental organizations.

Many of them may choose to become entrepreneurs in this sector as well.

MEFCC's interventions assume a major role in facilitating economic growth that is environment-friendly and sustainable while generating employment. These initiatives result in general improvement in the quality of life of people. The programs, and specific campaigns, have been launched to benefit the poorest of the poor and are inclusive.

It is fair to state that the ministry has been successful in ensuring significant outcomes as can be seen in the case of online monitoring of industrial waste.

Launching NAQI has resulted in creating widespread awareness among people living in cities who are now migrating to electric motor vehicles. Notable increase in forest and mangrove cover despite developmental imperatives is a matter of immense gratification for the current government. Wildlife populations (especially vanguard initiatives like Project Tiger) in the country have either stabilized or are increasing.

The ministry has launched several successful campaigns to connect with common people;educate them of the conservation measures through government schemes. The

use of technology in management and monitoring has yielded tangible results. Credit is due to MEFCC for facilitating sustainable economic growth by following a 'participative' approach.

MEFCC firmly believes that environment protection is a shared responsibility of the government and citizens. The ministry has shown to the world that sustainable development and environmental protection can be pursued simultaneously and are not disconnected objectives.

Based on the experiences of its officials, the ministry has listed out 'Green Good Deeds'. If each citizen does one environment friendly activity a day, there will be 130 billion green activities everyday which will have a transformative impact on environmental management.

However, much good work remains to be done. MEFCC's goals are a journey of collective learning and crowd-sourcing activities, and not a destination. The threat of environmental decline is faced not just by India by the entire world. MEFCC has been an active participant in the global conclaves and a signatory to far-reaching global agreements.

Some important issues that the MEFCC seeks to address immediately include

- clean air campaign in 100 cities

- creating greater opportunities for livelihood of coastal communities

- sustainable development and protection of coastal system

- planting trees by the billion to add 2.5 to 3 billion carbon stock

- National Forest Policy

- Finalization of 100 additional ESZ notifications

- development of cost-effective technologies for pollution abatement, climate change and biodiversity conservation

- Positioning India as the global leader in environment protection and sustainable development.

Picture Courtesy: Press Information Bureau (GOI)

Section 2
COP 26 : Tangible Action Plan

World leaders made a wide range of announcements at COP26 signalling a clear shift from ambition to immediate action. Countries , including India, made unprecedented commitments to protect forests, reduce methane emissions and accelerate green technology.

Amid powerful pleas heard in Glasgow, world leaders, young people and campaigners all stressed the urgency of taking tangible action to keep the prospect of holding back global temperature rises to 1.5 C and building resilience to climate impacts.

114 leaders took a landmark step forward at a convening of world leaders on forests by committing to halt and reverse forest loss and land degradation by 2030. The pledge is backed by $12bn in public and $7.2bn in private funding.

Countries from Canada to Russia to Brazil, China, Colombia, Indonesia and the Democratic Republic of the Congo all endorsed the Glasgow Leaders' Declaration on Forest and Land Use.

Together, they support 85% of the world's forests, an area of over 13 million square miles which absorbs around one third of global CO2 released from burning fossil fuels each year.

This announcement was bolstered with a commitment by CEOs from more than 30 financial institutions with over $8.7 trillion of global assets – including Aviva, Schroders and Axa – committing to eliminate investment in activities linked to deforestation.

COP 26, also the first time in recent history, hosted a major event on methane, with 103 countries, including 15 major emitters including Brazil, Nigeria and Canada, signing up to the Global Methane Pledge. This historic commitment, led by the US and EU alongside the UK COP26 presidency, equates to up to 40% of global methane emissions and 60% of global GDP.

More than 35 world leaders have also backed and signed up to the new Glasgow Breakthrough Agenda that will see countries and businesses work together to dramatically scale and speed up the development and deployment of clean technologies and drive down costs this decade. Signatories include the US, India, EU, developing economies and some of those most vulnerable to climate change – collectively representing more than 50% of the world's economy and every region.

The aim is to make clean technologies the most affordable, accessible and attractive choice for all globally in the most polluting sectors by 2030, particularly supporting the developing world to access the innovation and tools needed for a just transition to net zero.

Work will focus on five key sectors – power, road transport, hydrogen, steel and agriculture – which together represent more than half of total global emissions and further demonstrates how countries are moving from commitments to tangible action.

Leaders signed up to the Glasgow Breakthroughs also committed to discussing global progress every year in each sector starting in 2022 – supported by annual reports led by the International Energy Agency in collaboration with International Renewable Energy Agency and UN High Level Champions – and annual discussions of Ministers across government convened around the Mission Innovation and Clean Energy Ministerials. This 'Global Checkpoint Process' will seek to sustain and continually strengthen international cooperation across the agenda throughout this decade.

Leaders from South Africa, the United Kingdom, the United States, France, Germany and the European Union have announced a ground-breaking partnership to support South Africa with an Accelerated Just Energy Transition.

As a first step, the international partnership has announced that $8.5billion can be made available over the next 3-5 years to support South Africa - the world's most carbon-intensive electricity producer - to achieve the most ambitious target within South Africa's upgraded and ambitious Nationally Determined Contribution.

Alongside these strong signals from leaders, negotiators continued their crucial work on the systems and rules that underpin delivery. Early drafts of negotiating texts have been tabled on many issues and experts are working to find common ground, energised by the clear political direction from leaders.

COP26 President, Alok Sharma said:

"Forests are one of our best defences against catastrophic climate change, and essential to keeping 1.5C alive. This historic commitment will help end the devastating effects of deforestation and support the developing countries and indigenous communities who are the guardians of so much of the world's forests.

"The Glasgow Breakthroughs will help move us towards a global tipping point, where the clean, green technologies we need to reach net zero and keep 1.5C alive are more affordable, accessible and attractive for all than the polluting practices we are leaving behind.

"Today's launch of the Global Methane Pledge is also critical to keeping 1.5C alive. I am proud that COP has played host to a historic pledge which will play a vital role in limiting up to 0.2 degrees of warming across the next decade."

High-Level Climate Champions for COP25 and COP26, Gonzalo Munoz and Nigel Topping, said: "More than 18 sectors of the global economy have already achieved critical momentum, with key private sector actors mobilizing behind the breakthroughs necessary to achieve a net-zero world in time. Now, with more than 35 world leaders signing up to the Breakthrough Agenda, governments across the world will help dramatically scale and speed up the race to zero emissions and deliver the promise of the Paris Agreement. This is what the future of COP is all about - catalysing an innovative ambition loop between political leadership and

India & The United Nations

the dynamism of the private sector to drive towards a resilient, prosperous zero carbon future."

Also at COP26, world leaders, CEOs and philanthropists launched a series of new initiatives in support of the Glasgow Breakthroughs, including:

- The launch of the UK-India led Green Grids Initiative – One Sun One World One Grid, endorsed by over 80 countries, to mobilise political will, finance and technical assistance needed to interconnect continents, countries and communities to the very best renewable sources of power globally to ensure no one is left without access to clean energy.

- The Rockefeller Foundation, alongside IKEA Foundation and Bezos Earth Fund, launched the Global Energy Alliance for People & Planet with an initial $10 billion of funding from philanthropies and development banks to support energy access and the clean energy transition in the Global South, in strategic partnership with the UK-led Energy Transition Council.

- AIM4C, a new initiative led by the US and UAE, with over 30 supporting countries, committed to accelerating innovation in sustainable agriculture, having already garnered $4 billion in increased investment in climate-smart agriculture and food systems innovation, including $1bn from the US.

- The Breakthrough Energy Catalyst, headed by Bill Gates, programme aiming to raise $3bn in concessional capital to catalyse up to $30bn of investments in bring down clean technology costs and create markets for green products for green hydrogen, Direct Air Capture, long-duration energy storage and sustainable aviation fuel including £200m of UK support.

- The First Movers Coalition, a US-led buyers club of 25 major global companies making purchasing commitments to help commercialise key emerging clean technologies across hard-to-decabonise sectors like steel, trucking, shipping, aviation, aluminium, concrete, chemicals, and direct air capture

The COP26 meet of 2021 saw India, Thailand, Nepal, Nigeria and Vietnam make new net zero pledges which now means that 90% of the global economy is covered by net zero commitments. India's announcement also included a suite of ambitious 2030 commitments, including 500GW non fossil fuel power capacity, 50% energy requirements from renewable sources and 45% reduction of the carbon intensity of the economy. We've heard new NDC announcements from: Argentina, Brazil, Guyana, India, Mauritania, Morocco, Mozambique and Thailand and new Long-Term Strategies announced or submitted by Jamaica, Kazakhstan and the USA. On climate finance, we've seen new commitments from: Italy, Spain, Australia and Luxembourg.

Section 3

Net-zero, Aviation and Environment

UN climate champions have launched the Race to Zero Breakthroughs. It defines a roadmap with targets for over 20 key economic sectors, from aviation to steel production, to get to net-zero carbon emissions and slow the pace of climate change. Compiled below is the action plan of the aviation sector.

The International Air Transport Association (IATA), while welcoming the commitments towards strengthening climate action made at COP26, has called on the global efforts to decarbonize aviation to be supported with practical, effective government policies.

Management of international aviation's climate commitments sits outside of the COP process and is the responsibility of the International Civil Aviation Organization (ICAO). Nevertheless, airlines at the 77th IATA AGM in Boston, October (2021), agreed to achieve net-zero carbon emissions by 2050, in line with the stretch Paris agreement target to keep global warming to 1.5 degrees.

"Airlines are on the pathway to net-zero carbon emissions, in line with the Paris agreement. We all want the freedom to fly sustainably. Reaching net-zero emissions will be a huge task requiring the collective effort of industry and support from governments. The pledges made at COP26 show that many governments understand the key to rapid progress is to incentivize technological change and fund innovative solutions. This is particularly true of sustainable aviation fuels, which will play a major role in addressing aviation's environmental impact—they need the right incentives from governments to ramp-up production," said Willie Walsh, IATA's Director General.

India & The United Nations

A notable outcome from COP26 was the move by 23 nations to sign the International Aviation Climate Ambition Declaration. The Declaration recognizes the need for aviation to "grow sustainably" and reiterates ICAO's role to implement short, medium and long-term climate goals for the industry. Ensuring the maximum effectiveness of the Carbon Offsetting and Reduction Scheme for International Aviation (CORSIA), and the development and deployment of sustainable aviation fuels (SAF) are key aims of the Declaration.

"We are grateful to those states who have signed the International Aviation Climate Ambition Declaration and we urge more countries to commit to this initiative. The robust and realistic plan to fly net zero by 2050 agreed by our member airlines can be of great use to ICAO member states as they move forward with a global framework and long-term goal for aviation carbon reductions," said Walsh.

Scientific Understanding

ICAO Standards and guidance material on environmental issues are always founded on scientific consensus. As a consequence, in support of a data-driven decision making process, ICAO is constantly monitoring the evolution of scientific knowledge related to the impacts of aviation on the environment.

This is in line with provisions from the ICAO Resolution A40-17 (2019), where the ICAO Assembly invites States and international organizations to provide the necessary scientific information and data to enable ICAO to substantiate its work in this field; and encourages the Council to continue to cooperate closely with international organizations and other UN bodies on the understanding of aviation impacts on the environment and on the establishment of policies to address such impacts.

Climate Change

With a view to minimize the adverse effects of international civil aviation on the global climate, ICAO formulates policies, develops and updates Standards and Recommended Practices (SARPs) on aircraft emissions, and conducts outreach activities. These activities are conducted by the Secretariat and the Committee on Aviation and Environmental Protection (CAEP). In pursuing its activities, ICAO also cooperates with other United Nations bodies and international organizations.

The ICAO Assembly at its 40th Session in 2019 adopted Resolution A40-18: Consolidated statement of continuing ICAO policies and practices related to environmental protection — Climate change. It reiterated the two global aspirational goals for the international aviation sector of 2% annual fuel efficiency improvement through 2050 and carbon neutral growth from 2020 onwards, as established at the 37th Assembly in 2010.

To achieve the global aspirational goals and to promote sustainable growth of international aviation, ICAO is pursuing a basket of measures including aircraft technology improvements, operational improvements, sustainable aviation fuels, and market-based measures (CORSIA).

ICAO is also exploring the feasibility of a long-term global aspirational goal for international aviation, as

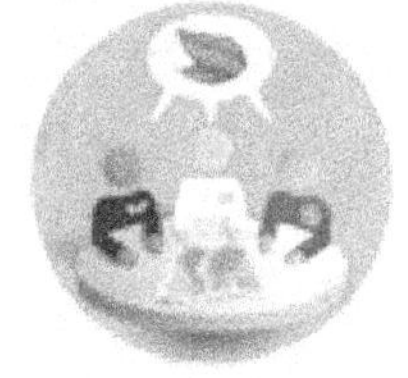

ICAO Tracker

CO_2 Emissions Reduction Initiatives

requested by the 40th Session of the ICAO Assembly (Reference: ICAO Assembly Resolution A40-18, paragraph 9).

Feasibility of a long term global aspirational goal for international aviation

In its 40th Session (2019), the ICAO Assembly requested the ICAO Council to continue to explore the feasibility of a long-term global aspirational goal for international aviation (LTAG), through conducting detailed studies assessing the attainability and impacts of any goals proposed, including the impact on growth as well as costs in all countries, especially developing countries, for the progress of the work to be presented to the 41st Session of the ICAO Assembly (2022). Assessment of long-term goals should include information from Member States on their experiences working towards the medium term goal (Reference: ICAO Assembly Resolution A40-18, paragraph 9)

In that regard, work is ongoing in ICAO to:

- Facilitate the involvement of relevant stakeholders outside the aviation sector to collect all information needed to support the exploration of the feasibility of a LTAG.
- Ensure that the best expertise is available for the assessment of the data, for the development of scenarios and for the assessment of the cost and benefits of scenarios.
- Keep ICAO Governing bodies informed and consulted during the process
- Ensure a transparent and inclusive process when consulting with States; and
- Provide a forum for the agreement of the possible options prior to the next ICAO Assembly.

Trends in Emissions that affect Climate Change

The first ICAO Global Environmental Trends were presented and endorsed at the 37th Session of the Assembly, and since then the updated global environment trends have been developed and presented to every Assembly Session to form the basis for their considerations and decisions.

As part of the CAEP/11 (2019) update to the ICAO Global Environmental Trends, a range of scenarios was developed for the assessment of future fuel burn and GHG emissions trends.

Fuel : International civil aviation consumed approximately 160 megatons (Mt) of fuel in 2015. By 2045, compared with an anticipated increase of 3.3 times growth in international air traffic (expressed in revenue tonne kilometres), fuel consumption is projected to increase by 2.2 to 3.1 times compared to 2015, depending on the technology and ATM scenarios. The long-term fuel burn from international aviation is lower by about 25% compared with the prior trends projections presented to the 39th Session of the Assembly. This lower fuel burn projection can be attributed to a combination of more fuel efficient aircraft entering the fleet, as well as a reduction in the forecasted long-term traffic demand. The 1.37% long-term fuel efficiency computed herein includes the combined improvements associated with both technology and operations. The individual contributions from technology and operations are 0.98% and 0.39%, respectively.

GHG : Significant uncertainties exist in predicting the contribution of sustainable aviation fuels in the future. However, a number of near-term scenarios evaluated by AFTF indicate that up to 2.6% of fuel consumption could potentially consist of sustainable aviation fuels by 2025. This analysis also considered the long-term availability of sustainable aviation fuels, finding that, by 2050, it would be physically possible to meet 100% of international aviation jet fuel demand with sustainable aviation fuels, corresponding to a 63% reduction in emissions. However, this level of fuel production could only be achieved with extremely large capital investments in sustainable aviation fuel production infrastructure, and substantial policy support. The effort required to reach these production volumes would have to significantly exceed historical precedent for other fuels, such as ethanol and biodiesel for road transportation.

Airports : Environmental issues relating to airport operations such as air and water quality, land management, noise, and climate change, has required States to respond with sound policies, plans and procedures. These include both voluntary and regulatory measures to achieve a balanced approach to environmental management. The compatibility of an airport with its environs can be achieved by proper planning of the airport, management of polluting-generating sources, and land-use planning of the area surrounding the airport.

ICAO have responded to these challenges through various initiatives:

ICAO CAEP Working Group 2 – Airports and Operations

CAEP WG2 has focused its work on the environmental aspects of airports and operations over the past 25 years.

Eco Airport e-collection

ICAO also fosters the exchange of information on best practices for Green Airports, covering such subjects as smart buildings, renewable energy, green mobility, climate change resilience resource and biodiversity protection, community engagement and sustainability reporting, with the aim of sharing and harmonizing best practices amongst airports. In that regard, ICAO has developed practical and ready-to-use information to support the planning and implementation of airport infrastructure projects. This is contained in the Eco-Airport e-collection under the form of a series of short publications.

Environmental Management, air quality and climate change mitigation at airports

As emerging issues require action, specific guidance material is developed by ICAO to identify, measure, and respond. The ICAO Doc 9184 – Airport Planning Manual – Part 2, Land Use and Environmental Management has formed the foundation on which proposed and operational airports can plan and manage the environment.

Additionally, air quality and climate change impacts are addressed in Doc. 10013 – Operational Opportunities to Reduce fuel Burn and Emissions and Doc. 9889 - Airport Air Quality Manual.

Balanced approach to aircraft noise Management

Airports are key stakeholders to improve practices on the ground. ICAO Doc. 9829 – Guidance Approach on the Balanced Approach to Aircraft Noise Management encompasses four principal elements: reduction of noise at source; land use planning and management; noise abatement operational procedures; and, operating restrictions on aircraft.

IPCC Reports

Specifically regarding aviation impacts on Climate Change, a comprehensive assessment concerning aviation's contribution to global atmospheric problems is contained in the Special Report on Aviation and the Global Atmosphere, which was prepared at ICAO's request by the Intergovernmental Panel on Climate Change (IPCC) in collaboration with the Scientific Assessment Panel to the Montreal Protocol on Substances that Deplete the Ozone Layer and was published in 1999. The conclusions of this report include:

- that aircraft emit gases and particles which alter the atmospheric concentration of greenhouse gases, trigger the formation of condensation trails and may increase cirrus cloudiness, all of which contribute to climate change; and

- that aircraft are estimated to contribute about 3.5 per cent of the total radiative forcing (a measure of change in climate) by all human activities and that this percentage, which excludes the effects of possible changes in cirrus clouds, was projected to grow.

The Report recognized that the effects of some types of aircraft emissions are well understood, revealed that the effects of others are not, and identified a number of key areas of scientific uncertainty that limit the ability to project aviation impacts on climate and ozone.

Global trends in Aircraft Noise

As part of the CAEP/11 (2019) update to the ICAO Global Environmental Trends, a range of scenarios was developed for the assessment of future noise trends. The noise indicators used are the total contour area and population inside the yearly average day-night level (DNL) 55 dB contours of 315 airports worldwide, representing approximately 80% of the global traffic.

Scenario 1 (CAEP/11 Baseline) assumes no further aircraft technology or operational improvements after 2015. Scenarios 2, 3, and 4 (low, moderate, advanced technology) assume that the noise levels of all new aircraft delivered after 2015 will reduce at a rate of 0.1, 0.2, and 0.3 EPNdB per annum, respectively. For all scenarios, an additional 2% reduction is applied to the population counts inside the noise contours, to reflect a possible improvement of aircraft routing around airports.

Figure 1 shows the total 55 dB DNL noise contour area from 2010 to 2050. In 2015, this area was 14,400 square-kilometres, and the population inside that area was approximately 30 million people. By 2045, the area is expected to grow from 1.0 to 2.2 times, compared with 2015, depending on the technology scenario. Of note is that under the advanced aircraft technology scenario (Scenario 4), from about 2030 onwards, the total yearly average DNL contour area may no longer increase with an increase in traffic.

The long-term total DNL 55 dB contour area is lower by about 10%, compared with the prior trends projections. This decrease can be attributed to a combination of quieter aircraft entering the fleet, as well as a reduction in the long-term traffic demand.

Technology Goals and Standards

To foster the development of new technologies, ICAO regularly sets technology goals, with the purpose of providing targets for industry research and development, in cooperation with States. Once the State of the Art of technology reaches these goals, consideration is given to updating the ICAO Environmental Standards to ensure the latest technologies are incorporated into aircraft and engine designs.

The ICAO Assembly Resolution A39-1 requests the Council, with the assistance and cooperation of other bodies of the Organization and of other international organizations, to continue with vigour the work related to the development of Standards, Recommended Practices and Procedures and/or guidance material dealing with the impact of aviation on the environment .

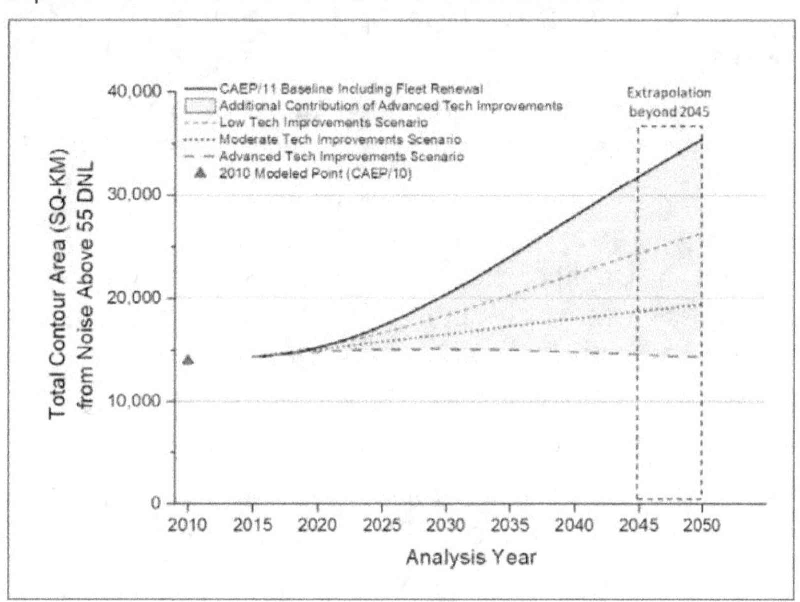

The ICAO has clearly articulated the environmental certification standards that shall be observed by aircraft and engine designs. The development and update of the environmental certification Standards ensure that the benefits offered by technology are reflected in real reductions of aviation environmental impacts, while balancing environmental benefit with technological feasibility, economic viability, and the interdependency between environmental factors.

The latest set of ICAO technology goals was developed by a panel of independent experts, which ensure transparency and involvement from all stakeholders. The results are detailed in the ICAO Doc 10127 - Independent Expert Integrated Technology Goals Assessment and Review for Engines and Aircraft. This was the first time that ICAO developed technology goals for noise, local air quality and CO2

emissions in an integrated manner, with full consideration of the interdependencies between the technologies.

(More details on this Independent Expert Review process and on the technology goals are provided in the ICAO Environmental Report 2019 (Chapter 1 – Aviation and the Environment: Outlook).

Land-use Planning and Management

Land-use planning and management is an effective means to ensure that the activities nearby airports are compatible with aviation. Its main goal is to minimize the population affected by aircraft noise by introducing land-use zoning around airports.

Compatible land-use planning and management is also a vital instrument in ensuring that the gains achieved by the reduced noise of the latest generation of aircraft are not offset by further residential development around airports.

ICAO continues to amend its policies on land use planning and management to minimize aircraft noise problems through preventive measures, to:

- locate new airports at an appropriate place, such as away from noise-sensitive areas;

- take the appropriate measures so that land-use planning is taken fully into account at the initial stage of any new airport or of development at an existing airport;

- define zones around airports associated with different noise levels taking into account population levels and growth as well as forecasts of traffic growth and establish criteria for the appropriate use of such land, taking account of ICAO guidance;

- enact legislation, establish guidance or other appropriate means to achieve compliance with those criteria for land use; and

- ensure that reader-friendly information on aircraft operations and their environmental effects is available to communities near airports;

ICAO manuals that provide guidance on the use of various tools for the minimization, control or prevention of the impact of aircraft noise in the vicinity of airports and describing the practices adopted for land-use planning and management by some States are available in public domain.

In addition, with a view to promoting a uniform method of assessing noise around airports, ICAO makes recommendations from time to time. Noise charges are also included as a possible noise management tool in the Balanced Approach. ICAO's policy with regard to noise charges was first developed in 1981.

The Council recognizes that, although reductions are being achieved in aircraft noise at source, many airports need to apply noise alleviation or prevention measures. The Council considers that the costs incurred may, at the discretion of States, be attributed to airports and recovered from the users. In the event that noise-related charges are levied, the Council recommends that they should be levied only at airports experiencing noise problems and should be designed to recover no more than the costs applied to their alleviation or prevention; and that

India & The United Nations

they should be non-discriminatory between users and not be established at such levels as to be prohibitively high for the operation of certain aircraft.

Practical advice on determining the cost basis for noise-related charges and their collection is provided in the ICAO Airport Economics Manual (Doc 9562) and information on noise-related charges actually levied is provided in the ICAO Manual of Airport and Air Navigation Facility Tariffs (Doc 7100).

Noise Abatement Operational Procedures

The way aircraft are operated in day-to-day operations may also present impacts in terms of the noise that reaches the ground. ICAO assists in the development and standardization of low noise operational procedures that are safe and cost-effective. The possibilities include noise preferential runways and routes and noise abatement procedures for take-off and landing. The appropriateness of any of these measures depends on the physical lay-out of the airport and its surroundings, but in all cases the procedure must give priority to safety considerations.

ICAO's recommendations on operational procedures are contained in several documents:

- Doc 8168 (Procedures for Air Navigation Services — Aircraft Operations (PANS-OPS)) Part I
- Doc 8168 (Procedures for Air Navigation Services — Aircraft Operations (PANS-OPS)) Part II
- Doc 9931 - Continuous Descent Operations (CDO) Manual and Doc 9993 - Continuous Climb Operations (CCO) Manual
- Doc 9888 – Review of noise abatement research and development and implementation projects
- Doc 10031 Guidance on Environmental Assessment of Proposed Air Traffic Management Operational Changes

Operating Restrictions

In the 1980s, the focus was on Non-Noise Certificated (NNC) aircraft; in the 1990s, it moved to Chapter 2 aircraft; today, it has moved to the noisiest Chapter 3 aircraft. However, operating restrictions of this kind can have significant economic implications for the airlines concerned.

The phase-out of NNC and Chapter 2 aircraft has already taken place in many ICAO contracting states. In the case of Chapter 3 aircraft, the ICAO Assembly in 2001 urged States not to introduce any operating restrictions at any airport on Chapter 3 aircraft before fully assessing available measures to address the noise problem at the airport concerned in accordance with the balanced approach. The Assembly also listed a number of safeguards that would need to be met if restrictions are imposed on Chapter 3 aircraft. For example, restrictions should be based on the noise performance of the aircraft and should be tailored to the noise problem of the airport concerned, and the special circumstances of operators from developing countries should be taken into account. This scheme has been ratified at the 39th Session of the Assembly .

Apart from phase-out, other possible operational restrictions include curfews, night time restrictions, noise quotas/budgets, cap rules, non-addition rules, and restrictions related to the nature of flight.

Noise from new aircraft concepts: New innovative technologies and energy sources for aviation are under development at a fast pace, and ICAO is closely following up these developments to prepare for their timely environmental certification, as appropriate. In that regard, ICAO is maintaining the E-HAPI, a website with a non-extensive list of ongoing projects that have been identified globally.

Specifically on aircraft noise, ICAO is following up possible environmental issues from the operation of unmanned aircraft, including remotely piloted aircraft and urban air mobility concepts.

Local Air Quality

One of ICAO's environmental goals is to limit or reduce the impact of aviation emissions on local air quality (LAQ). Starting during the late 1970s, ICAO has been developing measures to address emissions from aircraft engines in the vicinity of the airport and from relevant airport sources.

Following the latest successful adoption of the CAEP/10 nvPM Standard based on visibility criterion, CAEP/11 agreed on nvPM mass and number Standard, which will be considered for adoption by the ICAO Council.

ICAO provisions on LAQ also address liquid fuel venting, smoke (which is expected to be superseded by the nvPM Standard), and the main gaseous exhaust emissions from jet engines, namely: hydrocarbons (HC), oxides of nitrogen (NOx), carbon monoxide (CO).

Trends in Local Air Quality: As part of the CAEP/11 (2019) update to the ICAO Global Environmental Trends, a range of scenarios were developed for the assessment of future LAQ NOx and PM emission trends.

Scenario 1 for NOx and Scenario 1 for PM (CAEP/11 Baseline) assume no further aircraft technology or operational improvements after 2015. Scenarios 2 and 3 (moderate and advanced technology) for NOx assume aircraft NOx improvement based upon achieving 50 % and 100% respectively of the reduction from current NOx Emission levels to the NOx Emissions levels by CAEP/7 NOx Independent Expert (IE) goals review (-60 percent +/- 5 percent of current CAEP/6 NOx Standard) for 2036, with no further improvement thereafter. Scenario 2 for PM assumes only CAEP/9 IE Operational Improvement case.

The long-term LTO NOx projections are lower by about 2%, compared with the prior trends projections, due to a combination of aircraft with lower NOx engines, a reduction in the forecasted long-term traffic demand, as well as a refinement to the method used for computing LTO NOx.

Guidance on Airport Air Quality

ICAO recognizes that airport-related sources of emissions have the ability to emit pollutants that can contribute to the degradation of air quality of their nearby communities. As such, national and international air quality programmes and standards are continually requiring airport authorities and government bodies to address air quality issues in the vicinity of airports. Similarly, attention must also be paid to other possible airport-related environmental impacts associated with

India & The United Nations

noise, water quality, waste management, energy consumption and local ecology in the vicinity of airports, to help ensure both the short- and the long-term welfare of airport workers, users and surrounding communities.

One the initiatives that ICAO has undertaken to improve air quality is the creation and continued updating of the guidance Document 9889 "Airport Air Quality Manual". The manual provides guidance to assist with the assessment of airport emission sources, emission inventories and emissions allocation. The first step to addressing local air quality is to obtain an accurate estimate of the types and amounts of contaminants being introduced to the airshed. Then efforts to reduce these emissions can be pursued. The two main areas of an air quality assessment are: the emissions inventories; and the dispersion modelling of pollution concentrations.

An emissions inventory gives the total mass of emissions released into the environment and provides a basis for reporting, compliance, mitigation planning, and can be used as input for modelling pollution concentrations. In order to link emissions to pollution concentrations, the spatial and temporal distribution of the emissions have to be assessed as well. This combined approach of using emissions inventories and dispersion modelling enables the assessment of historical, existing and/or future pollution concentrations in the vicinity of airports or from individual emissions sources.

The emissions inventory, concentration modelling and ambient measurement elements of an air quality assessment can be used individually or in combination to aid the process of understanding, reporting, compliance and/or mitigation planning by providing information on overall conditions as well as specific source contributions. Subsequent air quality mitigation or other implemented measures (with proper consideration of the interrelationship with, primarily, noise and other airport environmental impacts) can have beneficial results for the total emissions mass, the concentration model results and measured concentrations.

Chapter 4

UN and Environment
-Environment - Definition and types
-Framework of Environmental Laws
-Environmental laws in India

Chapter-4
Framework of Environmental Laws in India

Consider the following:

- One billion people in the world have no clean water
- Two billion people worldwide have inadequate sanitation
- One and a half billion people globally (mostly in large cities of newly industrialized countries) breathe air that is dangerously unhealthy.

The situation is getting grimmer, if scientific studies are to be believed. Hence, the need for urgent action at all levels: individual, community and government.

It pays to remember that the planet will survive, and thrive, without humans. It is purely in the interest of the survival of the entire human race that we must act fast to mitigate the damage we have unleashed on this planet.

As we know, the term 'environment' refers to our surroundings that affect human life on Earth. Environment comprises the air we breathe, water that covers most of the planet's surface, and flora and fauna.. In recent years, scientists have undertaken to carefully study our interaction with the environment and have found that we have exploited, misused and abused the environment to our own detriment.

Humans are causing air pollution, deforestation, acid rain, and other climate changes dangerous both to the planet's ecosphere and humans. Governments, in the last few decades, have been keen to protect and promulgate cardinal laws that abate the abuse of the environment by their citizens.

Defining 'Environment'

The word 'environment' is derived from the French word 'environner', which means 'to encircle' or 'surround'. The most suitable definition of environment is …. the aggregate of water, air and land and the interrelationships that exist among them with human beings, other living organisms, and non-living matter. The environment is a combination of living and non-living things and mutual interaction with each other that leads to the creation and sustenance of an 'ecosystem'.

Protection of the environment is a global issue that concerns all of humankind and is among the top priorities for governments across the world irrespective of their size, stage of development or ideology. The interaction between humankind and nature is so extensive that the question of environment protection has assumed gargantuan proportions, affecting humanity at large.

The term 'pollution' refers to 'irresponsible treatment' of our environment through human action (direct and indirect). Human interference in the environment causes extinction of species, climatic changes, exhaustion of minerals and damages thousands of other delicate natural processes that sustain life on the planet.

In short, humans cause an 'imbalance' in the natural processes (physical and chemical) that sustain life. The excessive production of 'Greenhouse Gases' has brought about drastic climatic changes.

Addition of foreign material to water, air, and soil, may change the natural properties of these basic constituents that sustain life on the planet. Industrialization, poverty, population-explosion, urbanization, and over-exploitation of resources are some of the factors that have contributed to environmental deterioration, which is compounded by human greed.

Water Pollution

Water pollution is the contamination of water bodies (lakes, rivers, oceans, aquifers, and groundwater). Water pollution occurs when pollutants are discharged into water bodies by households and industries without adequate treatment to remove harmful compounds.

Source: iStock Free Pictures

Air Pollution

The air we breathe contains a mixture of various gases like Oxygen, Nitrogen, Carbon Dioxide, Argon etc. Air pollution is defined as the release of chemicals, particles, or biological materials into the atmosphere that cause discomfort, disease, or death.

Picture Courtesy: : National Institute of Open Schooling

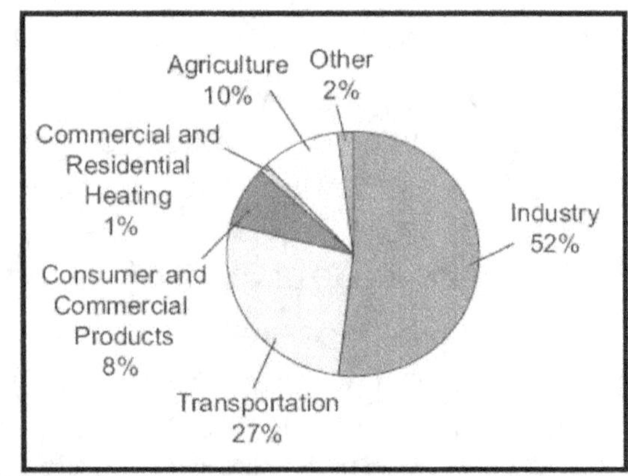

India & The United Nations

Share of air pollution by percentage in India

The major sources of air pollution are:

- Industrial emissions
- Vehicular emissions
- Domestic emissions

Common air pollutants in urban areas include Sulphur Dioxide (SO_2), Nitrogen Oxides (NO & NO_2), and Carbon Monoxide (CO). Gases discharged by refrigerators; air conditioners are responsible for depletion of the Ozone layer. This triggers harmful ultraviolet radiation from the Sun affecting people and other living organisms on Earth.

When Chlorine and Bromine atoms encounter the Ozone layer in the Stratosphere, they destroy Ozone molecules. One Chlorine atom can destroy over 100,000 Ozone molecules before it is removed from the Stratosphere. Compounds that release Chlorine or Bromine and cause Ozone depletion, are called Ozone-Depleting Substances (ODS).

Chlorofluorocarbons (CFCs), Hydrochlorofluorocarbons (HCFCs), Carbon Tetrachloride, and Methyl Chloroform are common ODS. Bromine, including Halons and Methyl Bromide are also common ODS. Although ODS are emitted at the Earth's surface, they are eventually carried into the Stratosphere in a process that can take as long as two to five years.

Noise Pollution

'Noise' is any sound that disrupts environmental equilibrium. A major source of 'noise' is by motor vehicles, aircraft, firecrackers, sirens, loud-speakers, and machinery. According to a survey conducted by the National Physical Laboratory, Delhi, Mumbai, and Kolkata are amongst the noisiest cities in the world. Noise pollution has harmful effects on the environment, humans, and animals. Some adverse effects of noise pollution on human health are:

- Hearing loss or hearing impairment
- Rise in blood pressure
- Cardio-vascular health effects
- Increase in stress level
- Decrease in efficiency and concentration

Noise pollution is excessively displeasing to humans, and animals alike. Machine-created environmental noise disrupts environmental balance.

Source: Internet

The source of most outdoor noise worldwide is mainly construction and transportation systems (including noise from motor vehicles, aircraft, trains and engines). Poor urban planning where industrial and residential buildings are in close proximity too contributes to noise pollution.

Land Pollution (and Solid Waste Pollution)

Deforestation, release of toxins into land, unhygienic waste, garbage, biomedical waste, and excessive use of fertilisers are all causes for land pollution. Unscrupulous use of pesticides is also a source of land pollution as it affects the potability of groundwater.

Solid waste pollution is a form of land pollution. Solid wastes include agricultural wastes, ashes, biomedical wastes, body parts of dead animals, dry and wet garbage from households that contain plastics, metals, wood, glass, paper, detergents. And also industrial and mining wastes.

Picture Source: Internet

Food Pollution (Food Adulteration)

The pollution of food begins by use of chemical fertilizers and pesticides at different stages of plant growth. These chemicals directly or indirectly affect the quality of food as well as the health of the consumer. Food also gets polluted during processing, storage, packaging, and transportation.Thermal Pollution

Atmospheric temperature plays an important role in determining the living conditions of organisms. Any undesirable, harmful change in natural temperature disturbs the natural heat balance. This is called 'Thermal Pollution'.

Nuclear (Radioactive) Pollution

Source: iStock Free Pictures

'Nuclear pollution" is caused through nuclear tests (for making nuclear weapons). Due to these explosions about 15% to 25% of the radioactive particles enter the atmosphere. They continue to fall back on the earth for several years. The Hiroshima Atomic Bombings is a harrowing example.

Environmental Protection

'Environmental protection' is the practice of protecting the natural environment at the individual, organizational or governmental levels. The rate of growth of the human population, and its interaction with nature, has resulted in a degraded biophysical environment. Governments have realized this and enacted laws restricting several activities that are harmful to the environment. Since the 1960's, several local, national and international

India & The United Nations

movements have attempted to create awareness about   environmental issues and challenges.

Source: Dreamstime.com

Academic institutions now offer courses on environmental laws, environmental studies, environmental management, and environmental engineering, and teach the history and methods of environment protection. Waste production, air pollution, and loss of biodiversity (resulting from the induction of invasive species and species extinction) are some of the issues related to environmental protection.

Environmental protection is a continuous and conscious process. It is influenced by three interwoven factors:

1. Environmental legislation
2. Ethics and
3. Education.

Each of the three influences the way we treat our environment. National-level environmental decisions and personal-level environmental values and behaviors are all equally responsible to undo the damage done by us over the years. For environmental protection to become a reality, it is important for societies to develop in each of these areas.

Environmental Law : what is it?

An environmental legal framework is essentially a set of laws and regulatory guidelines which regulate the relationships and conflicts between people and the environment.

The Supreme Court of India in K. M. Chinnappa v. Union of India defined "Environmental Law" as an instrument to protect and improve the environment, control, and prevent any act polluting (or likely to pollute the environment).

The Constitution of India clearly states that it is the duty of the state to "protect and improve the environment and safeguard forests and wildlife of the country". It makes it a duty of every citizen "to protect and improve the natural environment including forests, lakes, rivers, and wildlife". Reference to the environment has also been made in the Directive Principles of State Policy (Part IV) as well as the Fundamental Rights (Part III). The Department of Environment was established in India in 1980 to ensure a healthy environment for the country. This later became the Ministry of Environment and Forests in 1985.

Picture Courtesy: Los Alamos National Laboratory

Ministry of Environment, Forests and Climate Change (MEFCC)

The Ministry of Environment, Forests and Climate Change (MEFCC) is the nodal agency of the national executive established by the Central government for planning, promoting, coordinating and overseeing the implementation of India's environmental and forestry policies and programs.

The primary concerns of the ministry are implementation of policies and programs to conserve the country's natural resources. Included in its purview are the lakes, rivers, biodiversity, forests, and wildlife, ensuring the welfare of animals, and the prevention and abatement of pollution.

The broad objectives of the ministry are:

- Prevention and control of pollution
- Protection of the environment; and
- Ensuring the welfare of plants & animals

The 'Right to Life' mentioned in Article-21 of the Constitution of India includes the 'right to clean human environment'. Article-38 of our Constitution requires the state to ensure a social order for the welfare of people, which can be obtained by an unpolluted and clean environment.

Article-48A of the Constitution requires the state to adopt a 'Protectionist and Improvement Policy'. Protectionist policy imposes bans on things that lead to environmental degradation, (e.g. ban on use of leaded petrol, ban on use of plastic bags).

The Improvement policy refers to alternatives that can be used for improvement of environment, (e.g. use of CNG or low sulphur fuel, afforestation in industrial areas).

Article-48A of the Constitution declares: "The State shall endeavor to protect and improve the environment and safeguard forests and wildlife of the country."

Article-51A(g) of the Indian Constitution says: "It shall be the duty of every citizen of India to protect and improve the natural environment including forests, lakes, rivers and wildlife, and to have compassion for living creatures."

To balance ecology and economy and its sustainability, two main international conferences on the development of environmental law have been held. The first was Stockholm Conference, 1972, which is known as 'Earth Summit' and the Second International Conference was 'R10 Conference' on sustainable development popularly known as 'R10 Declaration' was held in 1992. The main objective of 'R10 Conference' was to strike a balance between ecology and economy and its sustainability.

(Picture Courtesy: lawlex.org)

Indian Perspectives

India has enacted laws to translate environmental imperatives and strategies into action. Laws have been promulgated to check water and air pollution for the safety and protection of forests and wildlife.

The global environmental crisis has questioned modernism and its values. The very existence and survival of all forms of life, including humankind, on the planet has become a matter of deep concern. The basic environmental principle is that "a good environment should be enjoyed by the present generation and bequeathed intact to the future generations".

In environmental law, 'Polluter-Pays-Principle' has been mandated to ensure responsibility and accountability. In simple words, the 'polluter' has to pay towards the costs of managing and preventing damage to human health or the environment." For instance, a factory that produces potentially poisonous substances as a by-product of its functioning is held responsible for safe disposal of its industrial waste.

Thomas Lindhqvist (Source: IIIEE website)

'Polluter Pays Principle' is also known as 'Extended Producer Responsibility' (EPR). This is a concept that was described by Thomas Lindhqvist, Senior Lecturer at the International Institute for Industrial Environmental Economics for the Swedish Government in 1990.

The credit for popularizing the 'Polluter Pays Principle' for the first time goes to the Organisation for Economic Co-operation and Development (OECD). The OECD defines EPR as ..."a concept where manufacturers and importers of products should bear a significant degree of responsibility for the environmental impacts of their products throughout the product life-cycle, including upstream impacts inherent in the selection of materials for the products, impacts from manufacturers' production processes itself, and downstream impacts from the use and disposal of the products."

Legislation for environmental protection in India

In tandem with the burgeoning of environmental consciousness, traditional approaches to environmental protection and improvement have undergone a paradigm shift. The downside of rapid industrialization and economic growth is under the lense .

Experts and governments are now examining how best to prevent this trade-off and reduce harm caused to the environment by economic activities. They have come to believe that environmental quality and economic advancement can be complementary.

The current spotlight on environment protection is not new in India. Environment protection has been an inherent part of Indian culture and traditions for eons. The need for conservation and sustainable use of natural resources has been delineated in Indian scriptures, over 3,000 years ago in the Vedas, and epics like Ramayana and Mahabharata. It is also highlighted in the Indian Constitution at many places.

Environment conservation and improvement is prominently addressed in the legislative and national policy framework as in the international agreements the country has been a signatory for. Even before India's independence in 1947, several environmental legislations existed but the real drive to put in place a robust legal framework came only after the United Nations (UN) Conference on the Human Environment (Stockholm, 1972).

India & The United Nations

Following the summit, the National Council for Environmental Policy and Planning within the Department of Science and Technology was set up in 1972. This Council later evolved into a full-fledged Ministry of Environment and Forests (MoEF; now called Ministry of Environment, Forests and Climate Change- MEFCC) in 1985 which today is the apex administrative body in the country for regulating and ensuring environmental protection.

After the Stockholm Earth Summit, 1976, constitutional sanction was given to environmental concerns through the 42nd Amendment, which incorporated them into the Directive Principles of State Policy and Fundamental Rights and Duties.

Former PM Indira Gandhi at the Stockholm Conference, 1972 (Source: nature.com)

Since the 1970s, an extensive framework of environmental legislations has been decreed in India. The MoEF (now known as MEFCC), and the state pollution control boards (CPCB i.e. Central Pollution Control Board and SPCBs i.e. State Pollution Control Boards) together form the regulatory and administrative core of the sector.

A policy agenda has also been developed to complement legislative provisions. The Policy Statement for Abatement of Pollution and the National Conservation Strategy and Policy Statement on Environment and Development were brought out by the ministry in 1992, to develop and stimulate initiatives for the protection and improvement of the environment.

The Environmental Action Programme (EAP) was formulated in 1993 with the purpose of expanding environmental services and combining environmental considerations in development programs and achieve sustainable development in several spheres of human economic activity. Several sector-specific policies have evolved, which are discussed in this chapter. This chapter endeavors to focus on legislative initiatives taken by the government in the field of environment protection and enhancement in the quality of life.

Water

Effluent Treatment Plant (Picture Courtesy: Pepprl+Fuchs)

Water quality standards (potability and brackishness) especially those for drinking water are set by the Indian Council of Medical Research (ICMR). These comply with World Health Organization (WHO) standards to a considerable extent.

The industrial effluents discharged into the land, lakes, rivers and other water bodies is regulated by the Indian Standard Codes. Of late, water quality standards for coastal water marine outfalls have also been specified. Additionally, specific standards have been stipulated for effluent discharges from iron & steel, aluminium, pulp and paper, oil refineries, petrochemicals, and thermal power plants. Legislations to control water pollution are listed below:

Water (Prevention and Control of Pollution) Act, 1974

This Act represented India's first attempt to comprehensively deal with land and water body pollution woes. The Act prohibits the discharge of pollutants (urban sewage and industrial effluents) into water bodies beyond a given standard. It stipulates penalties for non-compliance.

The Act was amended in 1988 to conform to the provisions of the EPA, 1986. It set up the Central Pollution Control Board (CPCB) which enforces standards for the prevention and control of water pollution. At the state- level, the State Pollution Control Boards (SPCBs) function under the direction of the CPCB and the state government.

The 1974 Act provided for the prevention and control of water pollution and maintaining the purity and potability of water (especially groundwater and aquifers). Though 75 per cent of the planet is covered with water, drinking water is the sparsest natural resource. Water being the largest ingredient needed for physiological processes of humans, animals, and plants, is the rarest commodity. Purification and supply of water involves heavy costs.

The 1974 Act was the first environmental preservation and management law passed in India. Its goal was to ensure that the domestic and industrial pollutants are not discharged into rivers, lakes, and other natural water bodies without adequate treatment. The reason is that such discharges render the water unsuitable for drinking and irrigation. They also destroy marine life result in the extinction of hundreds of marine species; and this also hits economic activities like fisheries hard.

Pollution Control Boards at the Centre and state were created to outline and enforce standards for factories discharging pollutants into water bodies using the 'Polluter-Pays-Principle'.

Water (Prevention and Control of Pollution) Cess Act, 1977

This Act enables governments and municipalities to levy and collect a cess on water consumed by industries and urban citizens. It targets augmenting CPCB's and SPCBs' financial resources needed to prevent and control of water pollution. Sewage

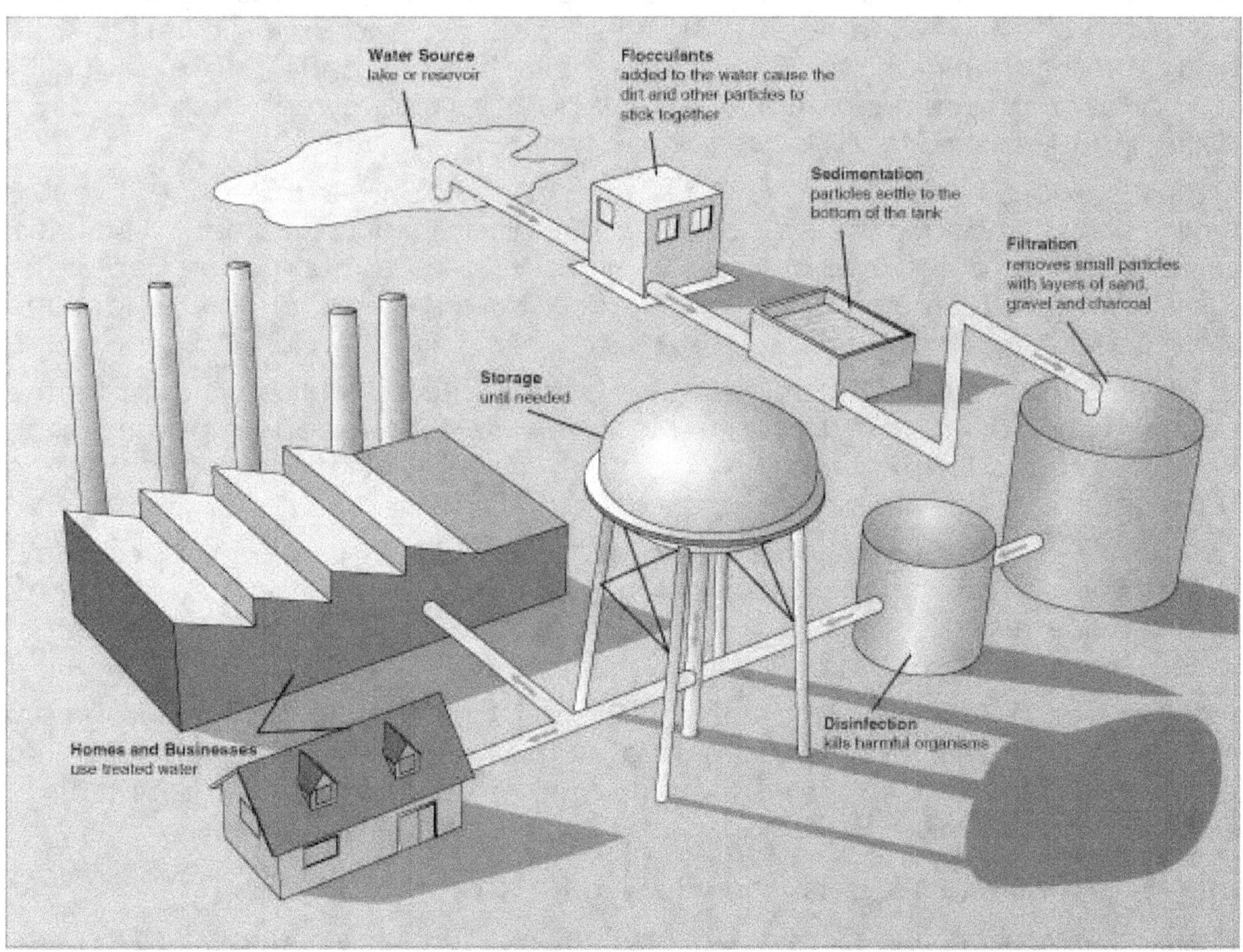

Treatment Plant (STP). (Picture Courtesy: SkyFi Labs)

In the wake of this Act, The Water (Prevention and Control of Pollution) Cess Rules were formulated in 1978 to identify indicators for the kind of and location of water meters that each consumer of water is required to install.

Air

Air pollution can be defined as an alteration in air quality that can be characterized by measurements of chemical, biological, or physical pollutants in the air. Air pollution refers to the undesirable presence of impurities or the abnormal rise in the proportion of some constituents of the atmosphere. It can be classified in two categories—'Visible' and 'Invisible' air pollution. Air pollution may also be categorized as:

- **Local:** The quality of ambient air within a radius of a few kilometres.
- **Regional:** Pollution like acid rain, photochemical reactions, and degradation of water quality at distances of a few kilometres to 1,000 kilometres
- **Global:** Depletion of the Ozone layer and global warming caused by the emission of Greenhouse Gases, mainly carbon dioxide (CO_2).

In the past four decades, India has passed many laws to control air pollution. As northern India suffers another air pollution emergency, it is yet another year of reckoning for the law that is all but forgotten. Air pollution laws aim to enable the "preservation of the quality of air and control of air pollution."

To fulfil India's commitments at the 1972 United Nations environment conference, laws have been enacted since 1981. These laws give sweeping powers to state and Central governments to punish and penalize polluters and improve air quality. They give the government teeth to enforce pollution control measures, shut down errant industries, and send polluters to jail.

Over the years, however, the law has seen a decline in its relevance, even as Indian cities climbed to top positions in global air pollution assessments, the latest being the State of the Global Air 2020. Almost zero cases have been filed under the Air Act from northern Indian states in recent years, even though they face the worst pollution every winter.

Even the Supreme Court and governments have ignored the laws that make the country a healthier place to live in. Measures like the Graded Response Action Plan or the Odd-Even scheme rely on other laws or regulations, some of which have nothing to do with the environment.

The Air Acts are commonly described as "toothless". As pollution spikes in the winter season, parliamentarians, lawyers, and activists demand amendments and replacements to obsolete laws. The year 2020 was the Solicitor General of India's turn to make a similar promise.

On October 28, 2020, GOI enacted the Commission for Air Quality Management in National Capital Region (NCR) and Adjoining Areas Ordinance (2020) to establish a panel to coordinate the air pollution between state governments of Delhi, Haryana, Punjab, Rajasthan, and Uttar Pradesh.

Air (Prevention and Control of Pollution) Act, 1981

The Air (Prevention and Control of Pollution) Act, 1981 was enacted to provide for the prevention, control, and abatement of air pollution in India. It is a specific

India & The United Nations

legislation that was enacted to take appropriate measures for the conservation of natural resources. They include the maintenance of air quality and air pollution control.

The principal objectives of the Act are:

- Prevention, control, and abatement of air pollution
- Setting up of central and state pollution control boards
- Maintenance of air quality in cities.

The 1981 Act was viewed as a solution to problems pertaining to air pollution, and ambient air quality standards established under it. The Act seeks to tackle and reduce air pollution by prohibiting the use of polluting fuels, and by regulating appliances that cause air pollution.

Under the Act, setting up and operating an industrial plant requires permits from SPCBs. The pollution control boards are also expected to test the air in designated areas, inspect pollution control equipment, and manufacturing processes.

National Ambient Air Quality Standards (NAAQS) for major pollutants were notified by the CPCB in April 1994. These are considered permissible levels of ambient air quality essential for healthy urban life. They consist of an adequate margin of safety, to protect public health, vegetation, and property.

The NAAQS prescribes specific standards for industrial, residential, rural, and other sensitive areas. Industry-specific emission standards have also been drawn up for iron and steel, cement, fertilizer plants, oil refineries and the aluminium industry. The ambient quality standards prescribed in India are similar to those prevailing in many developed and developing countries.

Picture Courtesy: World Health Organization (WHO)

To further empower the central and state pollution boards, the Air (Prevention and Control of Pollution) Amendment Act, 1987, was enacted.

The boards were allowed unilaterally by statute to take immediate measures to tackle emergent issues and recover the expenses incurred from offenders. The power to repeal the consent for non-fulfilment of the conditions prescribed has been emphasized in the Air Amendment Act.

The Air (Prevention and Control of Pollution) Rules formulated in 1982, defined the procedures for conducting meetings of the boards, the powers of the presiding officers, decision-making, quorum and other details to eliminate all ambiguities. They also prescribed the manner and purpose of seeking assistance from specialists and the fee to be paid thereof.

Complementing the above Acts is the Atomic Energy Act of 1982, which was introduced to tackle radioactive waste. In 1988, the Motor Vehicles Act, was enacted to regulate vehicular traffic, besides ensuring proper packaging, labelling and transportation of hazardous wastes.

(Picture Courtesy: iStock Free Pictures)

Various aspects of vehicular pollution have also been notified under the EPA of 1986. Mass emission standards were notified in 1990 and made more stringent in 1996.

In 2000, these standards were revised again. Separate obligations for vehicle owners, manufacturers and enforcing agencies were stipulated. In addition, stringent Euro I and II emission norms were notified by the Supreme Court on April 29, 1999, for the city of Delhi. The notification made it mandatory for car manufacturers to conform to the Euro I and Euro II standards by May 1999 and April 2000, respectively, for new non-commercial vehicles sold in Delhi.

Forests and wildlife

A forest is an earthly ecosystem, where plant and animal species (including human beings) interact with one another and with the physical environment. Countries differ in their forest cover, which in turn depends on various factors such as climate (rainfall and atmosphere temperature), availability of land, and population density.

Forests are crucial for maintaining the quality of the natural environment on the planet. The commercial benefits accruing from the forests include tangible products such as fuel wood, timber, fodder, manure and other non-timber and minor forest products like fruits, flowers, and honey. Millions are dependent on forests for their livelihood and subsistence.

Forests, however, serve a far more important role as saviours of life. Intangible processes such as moderating the hydrological cycle, soil conservation, climate change mitigation and wildlife habitat, and other intangibles such as spiritual, recreational, and aesthetic values also require preservation of forests and wildlife.

Indian Wildlife Species (Picture Courtesy: wildnest.com)

India is the seventh largest country in the world covering 2.4 per cent of the world area. However, only 1.8 per cent of forest cover is found in India. Despite recent efforts to increase forest cover through afforestation carried out mainly under Compensatory Afforestation Management and Planning Authority (CAMPA), India's forests are in a pitiable condition, with just over 21 per cent of India under forest cover in 2007, as stated in the State of Forest Report 2009 released by the Union Minister of Environment and Forests.

Dense forests (equatorial mangroves) cover only 12 per cent of the total land area. The policy requirement is that the forest cover should be 33 per cent of the country's area; and it should be 'closed'. However, India is far from achieving this number.

Indian Forests under Threat

Indian forests are in peril today and are reducing at an alarming rate due to the rapid human and livestock population explosion. Over-utilization and exploitation of natural resources, conversion of forest land for non-forestry purposes like agriculture, and other illegal activities such as logging, poaching, and unauthorized occupation of forest land are threatening the survival of forests in India.

Systematic management of forests began in the mid-nineteenth century. The first Indian forest policy promulgated in 1894 focused on commercial exploitation of timber and stressed permanent cultivation.

The 1952 revision of the policy put forth that one-third of the land area of the country should be under forest and tree cover. The Forest policy of 1988 focused on environmental stability and maintenance of ecological balance.

Until 1976, forest and wildlife were state subjects. Forest departments regulated forests in accordance with the Forest Act of 1927. Recognizing the significance of forests and wildlife, the 42nd Amendment to the Constitution deleted forest and environmental conservation from the state list and included them in the concurrent list, bringing them under the purview of both the Central and state governments. Now, Centre and states may legislate on issues pertaining to forests and protection of wildlife.

The 42nd Amendment also introduced a new Directive Principle of State Policy [Article 48-A] and a Fundamental Duty [51 (A) (g)] for the protection and improvement of the forests. These provisions provide are:

- Article 48-A – "Protection and improvement of environment and safeguarding of forests and wildlife". The state shall endeavour to protect and improve the environment and to safeguard the forests and wildlife of the country.

- Article 51 (A) (g) – "It shall be the duty of every citizen of India to protect and improve the natural environment including forests, lakes, rivers and wildlife, and to have compassion for living creatures."

(Picture Courtesy: homegrown.com)

India & The United Nations

Forest Conservation and Legal Action

"Prior to the British occupation of India, the customs and traditions of the Indian people had regulated the exploitation of forest resources in India. Certain types of trees were deemed sacred (egs. Banyan, Pipal) and never chopped down. They were allowed to grow for centuries and proliferate through the entire forest. Certain portions of forest cover were regarded as 'God's groves' ('Devara Kaadu' in local parlance), and even deadwood and leaves remained untouched by human hands in these areas (Gadgil M, Vartak V.D., 1981).

The history of Indian modern forest legislation is over 100-years old. The first codification in relation to Indian forest administration was the Indian Forest Act, 1865. It authorized the British government to confiscate land covered with trees as 'government owned forests' and manage them. The existing rights of individuals and communities were not to be impinged upon as the Act did not cover private forests.

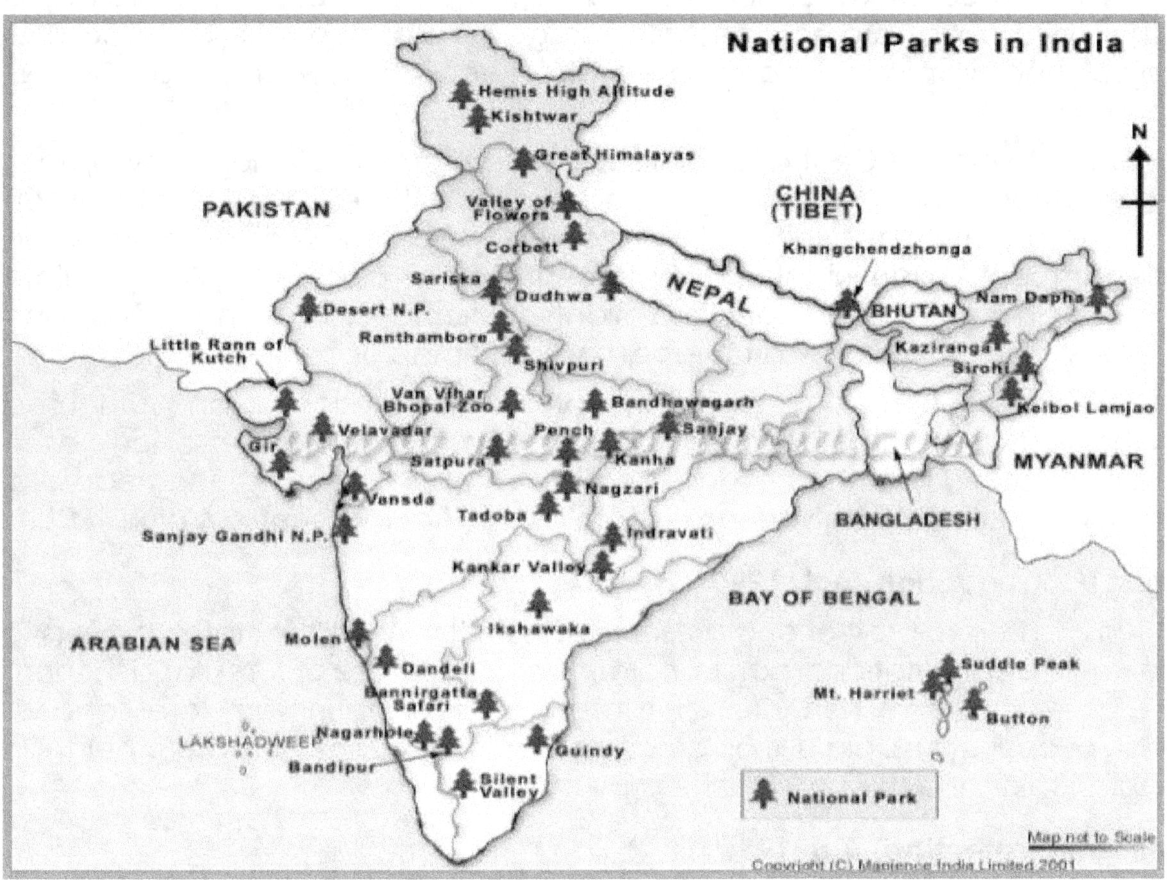

Source: Pinterest.com

The 1865 Act was replaced by a broader Indian Forest Act of 1878. Forests were categorized as Reserve Forests, Protected Forests and Village Forests. Many restrictions were imposed upon the people's rights over forest land and its resources exploitation in the Protected and Reserved Forests. The Act hugely changed the nature of common property, making it government property.

The Act was amended many times but was finally revoked and replaced by the Indian Forest Act, 1927.

The Forest and Wildlife Legislations currently in force in India are:

- The Indian Forest Act, 1927
- The Wildlife Protection Act, 1972
- The Forest Conservation Act, 1980
- The Scheduled Tribes and other Traditional Forest Dwellers Act, 2006

The Indian Forest Act, 1927

The passage of the Wildlife (Protection) Act, 1972, (Amendment 1991) was a significant milestone in the history of wildlife protection measures in India.

The WPA (Wildlife Protection Act), 1972, enables the special protection accorded to a large list of Indian wildlife species (flora and fauna). The 1972 Act applies to wildlife habitat conservation too. Ecologically important areas are protected under the Act. Habitat protection forms a large part of conservation measures (eg. Project Tiger involves preservation of the tiger habitat consisting of forest cover and tiger prey).

The WPA empowers the Central and state governments to declare any area a 'wildlife sanctuary', 'national park' or 'closed area'. There is a blanket ban on carrying out industrial activity within protected areas. The Act empowers the Forest department to administer and implement the provisions of the Act; regulate hunting wild animals; protect specified plants, sanctuaries, national parks, and closed areas; restrict trade or commerce in wild animals or animal articles.

The Act prohibits hunting of animals except with permission of an authorized officer when an animal has become dangerous to human life or property or so disabled or diseased as to be beyond recovery (WWF-India, 1999). The near-total prohibition on hunting was given more teeth by the Amendment Act of in 1991.

The Forest (Conservation) Act, 1980

This Act was passed to protect and preserve forests. It restricts the state's powers to 'de-reserve' or delimit national parks and reserve forests. Use of forestland for non-forest purposes (the term 'non-forest purpose' includes clearing any forestland for cultivation of cash crops, plantation crops, horticulture, or any purpose other than re-afforestation) is also severely checked by this Act.

Environment (Protection) Act, 1986 (EPA)

EPA, 1986 is an umbrella legislation designed to provide a framework of laws for the co-ordination of Central and state authorities in forest and wildlife habit protection. The Act has been enacted under the Water (Prevention and Control) Act, 1974 and Air (Prevention and Control) Act, 1981.

Under this Act, the Center has overriding powers to take steps necessary to protect and improve the quality of the environment by setting standards for emissions and discharges into the human and aquatic eco-systems thereby regulating the positioning of industries, management of hazardous wastes, and protection of public health and well-being.

The Centre issues notifications under the EPA for the protection of ecologically sensitive areas and issues guidelines for rules that comprise EPA.

Some notifications issued under this Act so far are:

- Doon Valley Notification (1989) prohibits the setting up of an industry in which the daily consumption of coal/fuel is more than 24 MT (million tons) per day in the Doon Valley.

- Coastal Regulation Zone (CRZ) Notification (1991) regulates activities along the coastlines of the sub-continent. According to this notification, dumping ash or other wastes in the CRZ is banned. Thermal power plants employing foreshore facilities for transport of raw materials, facilities for intake of cooling water and outfall for discharge of treated wastewater/cooling water) require clearance from the MEFCC.

- Dhanu Taluka Notification (1991), under which the district of Dhanu Taluka falls, has been declared an 'ecologically fragile' region and setting up power plants in its vicinity is forbidden.

- Revdanda Creek Notification (1989) prohibits establishment of industries in the belt around the Revdanda Creek.

- The Environmental Impact Assessment of Development Projects Notification, (1994 and as amended in 1997). As per this notification:

    1. All projects listed under Schedule One require environmental clearance from MEFCC.

    2. Projects under the de-licensed category of the New Industrial Policy also require clearance from MEFCC.

    3. All development projects whether under the Schedule One or not, if located in fragile regions, must obtain MEFCC clearance.

    4. Industrial projects with investments above Rs 500 million must obtain MEFCC clearance and are required to obtain a LOI (Letter of Intent) from the Industries Ministry, and an NOC (No Objection Certificate) from the SPCB and the State Forest Department if the location is on or near forestland. Once the NOC is obtained, the LOI is converted into an industrial license by the state authority.

    5. The notification stipulates procedural requirements for the setting up of and operation of new power plants. As per this notification, two-stage clearance for site-specific projects such as pithead thermal power plants and valley projects is required. Site clearance is given in the first stage and final environmental clearance in the second. A public hearing has been made mandatory for projects covered by this notification. This is an important step in providing transparency and a greater role to local communities.

    6. Ash Content Notification (1997) requires the use of beneficiated coal with ash content not exceeding 34 per cent with effect from June 2001, (the date later was extended to June 2002). This applies to all thermal plants located beyond 1,000 kilometers from the pithead and any thermal plant located in an urban area or, sensitive area irrespective of the distance from the pithead.

7. Taj Trapezium Notification (1998) stipulates that no power plant can be set up within the geographical limit of the Taj Trapezium assigned by the Taj Trapezium Zone Pollution (Prevention and Control) Authority.

8. Disposal of Fly Ash Notification (1999). The principal purpose of this notification is to conserve the topsoil, protect the environment and prevent the dumping and disposal of fly ash discharged from lignite-based power plants. The sterling feature of this notification is that no person within a radius of 50 km from a coal-or lignite-based power plant shall manufacture clay bricks or tiles without mixing at least 25 per cent of ash with soil on a weight basis. For the thermal power plants the utilization of the fly ash would be as follows:

    - Every coal and lignite-based power plant must supply fly ash for at least 10 years for the purpose of manufacturing ash-based products like cement, concrete blocks, bricks, and panels for construction of roads, embankments, dams, dikes etc.

    - Every coal and lignite-based thermal power plant, to obtain environmental clearance, must submit an action plan for complete utilization of fly ash. The plant, within a period of nine years phase out the dumping and disposal of fly ash on land in accordance the plan

9. Rules for the Manufacture, Use, Import, Export and Storage of Hazardous Micro-organisms/Genetically Engineered Organisms or Cells.

These rules were introduced in 1989 with the objective of protecting nature, and public health. They relate to stem cell research and gene technology (also micro-organism development), under the Environmental Protection Act, 1986.

The government in 1991, instituted a national label scheme for environment-friendly products called the 'ECOMARK'. The move attempts to incentivize manufactures and importers to reduce adverse environmental impacts, reward genuine R&D by companies to improve the quality of the environment and sustainability of resources.

Notifications relating to Recycled Plastics Manufacture and Usage Rules, 1999 were also constituted under the Environment (Protection) Act of 1986.

Environment (Protection) Rules, 1986

These rules specify the procedures for establishing emission or discharge standards of pollutants. The rules prescribe the limits for under which the Centre can issue prohibition orders, location restrictions and operation parameters for industries that emit or produce pollutants.

The rules provide for collecting samples, serving notice, submitting samples for analysis and formats for lab reports. The laboratories function as described by the rules and the qualifications required for of the lab technicians is also detailed in the rules.

National Environment Appellate Authority Act, 1997

This Act resulted in the establishment of a National Environment Appellate Authority to hear appeals in respect of restriction of areas in which industries may operate.

The Authority also hears pleas pertaining to industry classification, processes that industries are not allowed to put into operation (because they are subject to controls imposed under the Environment (Protection) Act, 1986).

Various acts specific to the coal sector have been enacted. The early attempts in this regard can be traced back to the Mines Act, 1952, which promoted health and safety standards for coal miners. Later the Coal Mines (Conservation and Development) Act (1974) was promulgated for the conservation of coal during mining operations. For conservation and development of oil and natural gas resources a similar legislation was enacted in 1959.

Hazardous wastes

There are several laws that completely or indirectly deal with hazardous waste. The relevant legislations are the Factories Act, 1948, the Public Liability Insurance Act, 1991, the National Environment Tribunal Act, 1995 and some notifications under the Environmental Protection Act of 1986.

Source: Wikipedia (Shutterstock.com)

Under the EPA 1986, the MEFCC has issued several notifications to tackle the menace and threat of hazardous waste. These include:

- Hazardous Wastes (Management and Handling) Rules, 1989, which presents guidelines for manufacture, storage and import of hazardous chemicals and for management of hazardous wastes.

- Biomedical Waste (Management and Handling) Rules, 1998, were formulated along parallel lines, for proper disposal, segregation, and transport of infectious wastes.

- Municipal Wastes (Management and Handling) Rules, 2000; these rules empower municipalities to dispose municipal solid waste in a scientific manner.

- Hazardous Wastes (Management and Handling) Amendment Rules, 2000 which is a recent notification issued to lay down guidelines for the import and export of hazardous waste in the country.

Factories Act, 1948 and its Amendment in 1987

The Factories Act, 1948 was a post-independence statute that explicitly demonstrated a concern for the environment. The primary aim of the 1948 Act has been to ensure the welfare of workers not only in their working conditions in the factories but also their employment benefits.

Simultaneously ensuring the safety and health of the workers, and protecting the environment, the Act aids environmental conservation. The Act contains a comprehensive list of 29 categories of industries adopting hazardous processes. These are defined as a process or activity where unless special care is taken, raw materials used or the intermediate and the finished products, by-products, wastes or effluents would:

- Cause material impairment to employees' health

- Result in the pollution of the environment

(Picture Courtesy: Pexels.com)

India & The United Nations

Public Liability Insurance Act (PLIA), 1991

The Act covers accidents involving hazardous substances and insurance coverage for workers. Where death or injury results from an accident, this Act makes the owner liable to provide relief as specified in the Schedule of the Act. The PLIA was amended in 1992, and the Central government was authorized to establish the Environmental Relief Fund, for making relief payments.

National Environment Tribunal Act, 1995

This Act provided strict liability for damages arising out of any accident occurring while handling hazardous substances and for the establishment of a National Environment Tribunal for effective and expeditious disposal of cases arising from accidents involving hazardous raw materials. Relief or compensation in case of accidents to be given to workers, environmental damages (including property damage) is guaranteed by this Act.

Indian Regulatory Framework for Environment Protection: An assessment

The Indian regulatory framework for environment protection and conservation is robust and this is evident in all that has been discussed above. However, implementation and execution of these laws/rules leaves a lot to be desired.

One commonly cited reason is the prevailing command and control nature of the environmental regime. Coupled with this is the prevalence of the all-or–nothing approach of the law. Laws do not consider the extent of violation. Fines are levied on a flat rate basis and there is no incentive to lower the discharges below prescribed levels.

Some initiatives have addressed these issues in the recent past. GOI brought out a Policy Statement for Abatement of Pollution in 1992, before the Rio conference, which declared that market-based approaches would be considered in controlling pollution.

It stated that economic instruments will be investigated to encourage the shift from curative to preventive measures, internalize the costs of pollution and conserve resources, particularly water.

In 1995, the MEFCC constituted a task force to evaluate market-based instruments, which strongly advocated the use for the abatement of industrial pollution. Various economic incentives have been used to supplement the command-and-control policies. Depreciation allowances, exemptions from excise or customs duty payment, and arrangement of soft loans for the adoption of clean technologies are instances of such incentives.

Another aspect that is evident is the shift in the focus from end-of-pipe treatment of pollution to treatment at source. The role of remote sensing and geographical information systems in natural resource management and environmental protection has also gained importance over time

A significant recent development is the rise of judicial activism in the enforcement of environmental legislation. 'Green Judges' have indirectly joined the environment protection movements and ruled in favor of public interest legislations (PILs) that seek to conserve the environment and mitigate its misuse/abuse.

This is reflected in the increasing number of environment-related public litigation cases that have led the courts to take major steps such as ordering the shutdown of polluting factories.

Agenda 21 highlights the need for integration of environmental concerns at all stages of policy, planning and decision-making processes including the use of an effective legal and regulatory framework, economic instruments, and other incentives. These very principles were fundamental to environmental protection in the country well before Rio and will be reinforced, drawing on India's own experiences and those of other countries.

Environmental Impact Assessment (EIA)

Recent rules effected in India favour a regimental environment management by the Union government. This move has both positives and negatives. While it makes for a robust centralized control and implementation mechanism, it weakens the federal structure and takes power and responsibility off the states. The proposed changes give the Union government full powers to appoint the State Environmental Impact Assessment Authority (EIA).

Laws like National Biodiversity Act, 2002, lend significant role and autonomy to local bodies such as Panchayat Raj institutions, in the protection and conservation of local biodiversity.

Decentralisation has helped lessen the damage done and given rise to

sustainable co-existence with local environments. Given these positive outcomes, it only makes sense for allied environmental laws to follow a similar 'grassroots' approach.

With EIA set to assume a key role in sustainable development from here on, there is a need to elevate its lawful importance from just an executive notification to a full-fledged Parliamentary act.

As a notification, the provisions get lesser legal binding and are liable to varying interpretations based on the whims of the local administrators.

As an enactment, it will fetch greater stability and uniformity in the EIA process. A parliamentary committee must be constituted to examine the scope and powers under such an act.

India has not only set grand goals in environment and climate change management at several international forums, but also taken a lead role in renewable energy in the form of the International Solar Alliance. Diluted domestic regulations seem inconsistent with these aspirations and the overall objective to be a global leader in the fight against environmental decline.

Environmental Impact Assessment (EIA) is a process of evaluating the likely environmental impacts of a proposed project or development, considering inter-related socio-economic, cultural, and human-health impacts (both beneficial and adverse).

The UN Environmental Program (UNEP) defines EIA as a tool used to identify the environmental, social, and economic impacts of a project prior to decision-making.

It aims to predict and preclude environmental impacts at a nascent stage in project planning and design, find ways and means to lessen adverse impacts, shape projects to suit the local environment and present the predictions and options to decision-makers.

EIA in India is statutorily backed by the Environment Protection Act, 1986 which contains various provisions on EIA methodology and process.

EIA in India

The Indian experience with EIA began decades ago. It started in 1976-77 when the Planning Commission asked the Department of Science and Technology to examine the river-valley projects from an environmental angle.

Till 1994, environmental clearance from the Central Government was an administrative decision and lacked legislative support. On January 27, 1994, the then Union Ministry of Environment and Forests, under the Environmental (Protection) Act 1986, promulgated an EIA notification making Environmental Clearance (EC) mandatory for expansion or modernisation of any activity or for setting up new projects listed in Schedule 1 of the notification.

The Ministry of Environment, Forests and Climate Change (MEFCC) notified new EIA legislation in September 2006. The notification makes it obligatory for various projects such as mining, thermal power plants, river valley, infrastructure (road, highway, ports, harbours, and airports) and industries including very small electroplating or foundry units to get environment clearance. However, unlike the EIA Notification of 1994, the new legislation has shifted the onus of clearing projects to the state government depending on the size/capacity of the project.

EIA Process

The EIA process is cyclical with interaction between the various steps as given below:

- Screening: The project plan is screened for investment proportions, location, and type of development and if the project needs statutory clearance.

- Scoping: The project's potential impacts, zone of impacts, mitigation possibilities and need for monitoring

- Collection of baseline data: Baseline data is the environmental status of study area.

- Impact prediction: Positive, negative, reversible, irreversible, temporary, and permanent impacts need to be predicted which presumes a good understanding of the project by the assessment agency

- Mitigation measures and EIA report: The EIA report should include the steps for preventing, curtailing the impacts, the compensation for probable environmental damage or loss

- Public Hearing: On completion of the EIA report, public and environmental groups living close to project site may be informed and consulted

- Decision making: Impact Assessment Authority along with the experts consult the project-in-charge along with consultant to take the final decision, keeping in mind EIA and EMP (Environment Management Plan).

- Monitoring and Implementation of Environmental Management Plan: The various phases of implementation of the project are monitored

- Assessment of Alternatives, Delineation of Mitigation Measures and Environmental Impact Assessment Report: For every project, possible alternatives should be identified, and environmental attributes tallied as against the presumed damages. Alternatives should cover both project location and process technologies.

Once alternatives have been reviewed, a mitigation plan should be drawn up for the selected option and is supplemented with an Environmental Management Plan (EMP) to guide the proponent towards environmental improvements. Inventory analysis and hazard probability and index also form part of EIA procedures.

Chapter 5

International Agreements and UN's Common Agenda

-International agreements

- Convention on International Trade in Endangered Species of wild fauna and flora (CITES), 1973
- Montreal Protocol on Substances that deplete the Ozone Layer (to the Vienna Convention for the Protection of the Ozone Layer), 1987
- Basel Convention on Transboundary Movement of Hazardous Wastes, 1989
- UN Framework Convention on Climate Change (UNFCCC), 1992
- Convention on Biological Diversity, 1992
- UN Convention on Desertification, 1994
- International Tropical Timber Agreement and The International Tropical Timber Organisation 1983, 1994

International Agreements and UN's Common Agenda

The newly appointed Secretary General of the United Nation Antonio Guterres in his acceptance speech said, the humankind was at an 'inflection point' in history. In our biggest shared threat since the Second World War, humanity faces a stark dilemma- it is now a 'breakthrough' or 'breakdown'.

(UN Secretary General Antonio Guterres) Source: UN website

COVID-19 has become a global healthcare threat for two years now with almost no respite in the spread of the pandemic. It has destroyed lives, economies  and livelihoods of people thereby laying waste all the good work that the UN and its member states had done to decrease social, economic, and cultural disparities among peoples across the world.

Conflicts between governments and their national enemies and terrorism continue to rage and worsen. The disastrous effects of climate change have resulted in placing over one million earthly species at the threat of extinction, caused floods, fires, and extreme heat. For millions the world-over, poverty, discrimination, violence, and exclusion are denying them their rights to the basic necessities of life, health, safety, inoculations against disease, drinking water, seat in a classroom or one square meal a day.

UN has on its hand the stupendous task of rebuilding a world that seems to have abandoned values like trust and solidarity. As people around the world wantonly ignore fundamental human rights, the UN needs to rebuild a secure, peaceful, and prosperous world with a sustainable future for all life on the planet. The future of humankind depends on the two core values of trust and solidarity. These are also the values that enable nations to work together to achieve common goals and shared agenda. These are the very values that make all of humanity one gargantuan family.

In 2020, as the UN celebrated its 75th anniversary, member states agreed that their challenges are interlinked, across borders and socio-economic-ideological divides. Such challenges can only be faced by an equally robust and interconnected response, through re-energized multilateralism with the United Nations at the core of such initiatives. Member states asked Secretary General Guterres to report back with recommendations to advance a common global agenda.

India & The United Nations

SOCIAL PROTECTION SYSTEMS ARE CRITICAL TO ACHIEVING THE SUSTAINABLE DEVELOPMENT GOALS

(Picture Courtesy: UN official website)

In his response, Guterres engaged with a broad array of stakeholders, including member states, thought leaders, youth, civil society and the United Nations system and its many partners. One message rang through loud and clear: the choices we make, or fail to make, today could result in further 'breakdown, or a breakthrough' to a greener, better, safer future.

"The choice is ours to make; but we will not have this chance again.

That is why Our Common Agenda is, above all, an agenda of action designed to accelerate the implementation of existing agreements, including the Sustainable Development Goals," Guterres stated.

"Now is the time to re-embrace global solidarity and find new ways of working together for the common good. This must include a global vaccination plan to deliver vaccines against COVID-19 into the arms of the millions of people who are still denied this basic life-saving measure. Moreover, it must include urgent and bold steps to address the triple crisis of climate disruption, biodiversity loss and pollution destroying our planet," he added.

Global stock-taking meeting

International leaders of the UN who are meeting ahead of the global stock-taking meeting in 2023, will commit to the 1.5-degree Celsius goal*and net zero emissions by 2050 or sooner. Declarations of climate emergency and right to a healthy environment will be deliberated at length.

(The Paris Agreement is a legally binding international treaty on climate change. It was adopted by 196 Parties at COP 21 in Paris, on 12 December 2015 and entered into force on 4 November 2016. Its goal is to limit global warming to well below 2, preferably to 1.5 degrees Celsius, compared to pre-industrial levels. To achieve this long-term temperature goal, countries aim to reach global peaking of greenhouse gas emissions as soon as possible to achieve a climate neutral world by mid-century.)

A support package for developing countries will be discussed and designed for implementation during 2022-23. Measures for adaptation and resilience among member nations hit hard by the pandemic will be delineated.

No new coal mining after 2021 and phasing out fossil fuel subsidies will be on the agenda. Auditing will be co-joined with economic models, carbon pricing mechanisms and credible commitments by financial actors. A post-2020 biodiversity framework will evolve at the meet. Transforming food systems for sustainability, nutrition and fairness will share the spotlight with other essential agenda items aimed at ending hunger and poverty.

The General Assembly will resolve to act on territorial threats of climate change and prevent, protect, and solve issues concerning environmental degradation. Owing to unchanged emission levels from human activity, global warming of 2°Celcius will be exceeded during the current century.

Heatwaves, floods, droughts, tropical cyclones, and other extremes are unprecedented in magnitude, frequency and timing and occur in regions that have never been affected before. The Arctic is ice free in the summer; most permafrost is lost, and extreme sea levels occur every year. One million species are on the verge of extinction, with irreversible biodiversity loss and over 1 billion people live with atmospheric heat that is unbearable.

The goal is to limit global temperature rise to 1.5°Celcius. All countries and sectors must decarbonize by 2050 and extend support to countries facing heightened climate emergencies. A just transition to a new labour ecosystem is imperative. . The UN aims to ensure that a functioning ecosystem is preserved for succeeding generations and communities build resilience to climate change.

Nearly 75 per cent of methane emissions can be mitigated with existing technology -- up to 40 per cent of it at no net cost. Seventy-five years ago, the world faced a series of disastrous events: two successive

cataclysmic world wars, the Holocaust and genocide in various restive nations, devastating influenza epidemic and a worldwide economic depression.

The United Nations' founders gathered in San Francisco vowing to save succeeding generations from the scourge of war; reaffirm faith in fundamental human rights, dignity and worth of human beings. They swore to establish equal rights for women and nations (however small or big) and to establish conditions under which justice and respect for international law is established and sustained to promote social progress and better life standards. They believed in the worth of collective efforts to make a better world.

Artic Icecap meltdown due to Global Warming (Picture Courtesy: National Geographic Society)

The United Nations Charter is an exceptional achievement. Since 1945, international norms and institutions have delivered independence, peace, prosperity, justice, human rights, hope and support for billions of people. For others, however, these aspirations were never fully realized. A large number of people continue to be excluded from the opportunities and benefits of technology; transitioning economies still face a bleak future.

The coronavirus (COVID-19) pandemic has been a challenge like no other (since the Second World War). It revealed our 'shared vulnerability'

and 'interconnectedness'. It has exposed human rights concerns and exacerbated deep fragilities and inequalities in our societies. It has amplified disenchantment with institutions and political leadership. We have also seen many examples of 'vaccine nationalism'.

Moreover, with less than a decade to go, Sustainable Development Goals have been thrown further off track. At the same time, the pandemic has led to a surge of collective action, bringing all of humanity together to respond to a truly global threat.

"The world needs to unite to produce and distribute sufficient vaccines for everyone. We have been reminded of the vital role of the state in solving problems, but also the need for networks of actors stretching well beyond states to cities, corporations, scientists, health professionals, researchers, civil society, the media, faith-based groups and individuals," declared Guterres and added: "Cooperation and solidarity are the only two solutions to the current crises."

International agreements in force

Brundtland Commission 1983

Post Stockholm, concerns for the environment continued to increase and expand across continents. There was widespread deforestation, industrial pollution, and environmental degradation. The ozone hole, the warming of the Earth, increased carbon dioxide in the environment all added to the growing environmental worries. A need was felt to link environmental concerns with industrial development (sustainability in development) and growth. Mindful of this, the United Nations, in 1983, established the *"World Commission on the Environment and Development"* referred to as the *"Brundtland Commission"*.

The Brundtland Commission Report – *'Our Common Future'* in 1987 defined *'Sustainable Development' as* "development that meets the needs of the present without compromising the ability of future generations to meet their own needs" ….is the accepted definition of Sustainable Development.

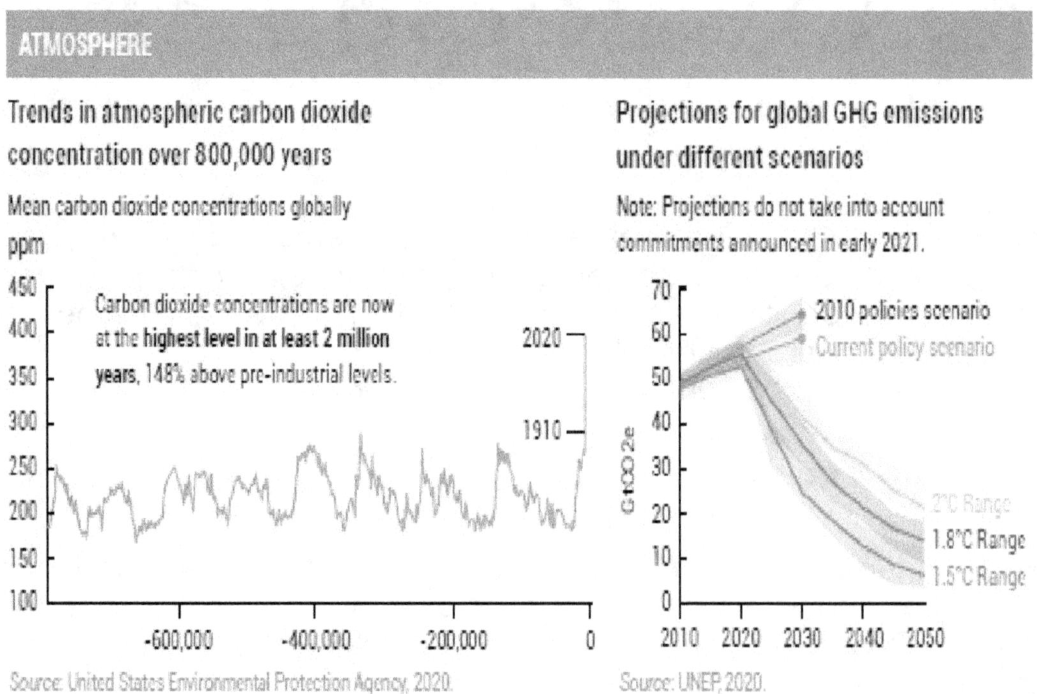

Rio Declaration 1992- Agenda 21

Twenty years after Stockholm, the United Nations Conference on Environment and Development was held in Rio de Janeiro in 1992. 'The Earth Summit', as it was called, adopted the 'Rio Declaration' and an action plan of 40 chapters called Agenda

India & The United Nations

21 by over 100 nations. Agenda 21 was geared towards achieving Sustainable Development in the 21st century. The 'Rio Concept' can be summarised as:

- Equal consideration of environment, society, and economy
- Intergenerational solidarity keeping in mind the needs of the future generations
- A global consensus and political commitment at the national and international levels
- Involvement of the Non-Government Organizations (NGOs)
- Provides a blueprint for the governments to attain a balance between the environment and the needs of the population; and
- A Commission on Sustainable Development (CSD) was established to follow up the Rio agreements, and it monitors the agreements of the Earth Summit at the local, national, regional, and international levels.

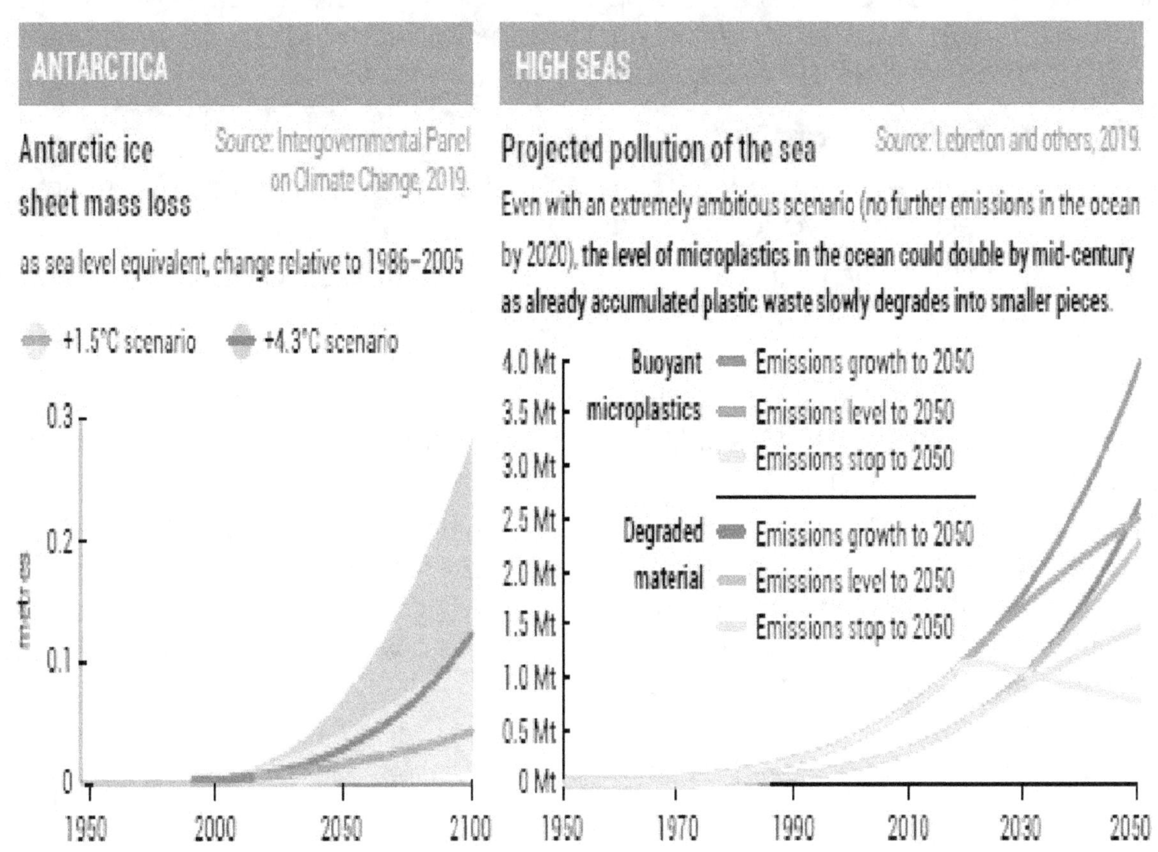

The Rio Summit Follow up

The Rio Summit was followed by several other conferences to focus on 'Sustainable Development'. These include:

- The Global Conference on Sustainable Development of Small Island Developing States in Barbados in 1994
- The World Summit on Social Development in Copenhagen in 1995
- The Fourth World Conference on Women, Beijing 1995;

- The Second UN Conference on Human Settlements, Habitat II, in Istanbul in 1996.

The imperatives were to follow the path of Sustainable Development in all countries in all parts of the ecosystem whether on land, water, or air. The effort was towards an all-inclusive development that cascades down to all sections of the population with special focus on the vulnerable sections like women, children or the marginalized.

A five-year review of the progress of the 'Earth Summit' was held in 1997 by the United Nations General Assembly. This was followed by a 10-year review in 2002 by the World Summit on Sustainable Development (WSSD). The WSSD was held in Johannesburg, South Africa. It urged the Nations to make progress in the formulation and implementation of strategies for sustainable development and to begin implementing them by 2005.

In 2000, the largest-ever gathering of world leaders agreed to a set of time-bound and measurable goals for combating poverty, hunger, disease, illiteracy, environmental degradation and discrimination against women, to be achieved by 2015. These are called the Millennium Development Goals.

Consensus for 'Earth Forward'

The following is a brief overview of a few significant decisions and agreements that were reached by the various countries:

- In 2004, Delhi (India) mandated the use of compressed natural gas in city buses and auto rickshaws, responding to rising pressure over air pollution complaints

- In 2005, Kyoto Protocol mandated a legal compulsion by which developed countries must enforce Greenhouse Gas emission reductions, by establishing the Clean Development Mechanism for developing countries.

- In 2007, Montreal Protocol was signed on substances that deplete the 'Ozone Layer' (ODS). Countries agreed to an accelerated phase-out schedule for hydro- chlorofluorocarbons (HCFCs). NASA has reported that the 'ozone layer' is recovering, in part due to reduced concentrations of CFCs, phased out under the 'Montreal Protocol'.

- In 2008, Green Economy ideas entered the mainstream. National Governments allocated more funds to further stimulate environmental actions and green growth figured among the new objectives for the future economy. Scientists documented the increasing acidification of oceans due to increasing levels of atmospheric Carbon Dioxide, which is predicted to have disastrous consequences for the earth's ecosystem.

- In 2009, Copenhagen Climate Negotiations were held. However, the participating countries failed to reach an agreement on new emission reduction commitments beyond 2012 (the end of the 'Kyoto Protocol' time frame). An important outcome of the meet however was the thrust on national and regional efforts to reduce emissions.

- In 2009, the G20 Pittsburgh Summit was held. Leaders called for making fossil fuels such as petrol and diesel more expensive to phase them out. They also agreed to provide targeted support for the poorest people.

- In 2011, Climate Change Negotiations were held in Durban. The outcome was a step forward in establishing an international agreement beyond Kyoto. It was agreed to cut carbon emissions in all countries, including developed countries and several major developing countries.
- In 2012, one of the first of the Millennium Development Goal targets achieved, in advance of the 2015 deadline. The percentage of the world's people without access to safe drinking water is cut in half.
- The 2012 United Nations Climate Change Conference was held in Doha. It was agreed to extend the 'Kyoto Protocol' that was to end in 2012 to 2020. It was also agreed to renegotiate the agreement reached in Durban by 2015 and to implement it by 2020.
- From the 'Stockholm Declaration' of 1972 to the latest Conference held in Doha in 2012, more than forty years have passed. The UN member nations are actively involved in greening the planet and developing clean energy solutions. The world is committed towards combating hunger, disease, illiteracy, poverty, reducing inequalities and so on. The target is to ensure that the benefits of development accrue to all sections of society and not at the cost of the future generations.

ENVIRONMENT

Ozone depleting emissions since the Montreal Protocol, Index 1986 = 100%

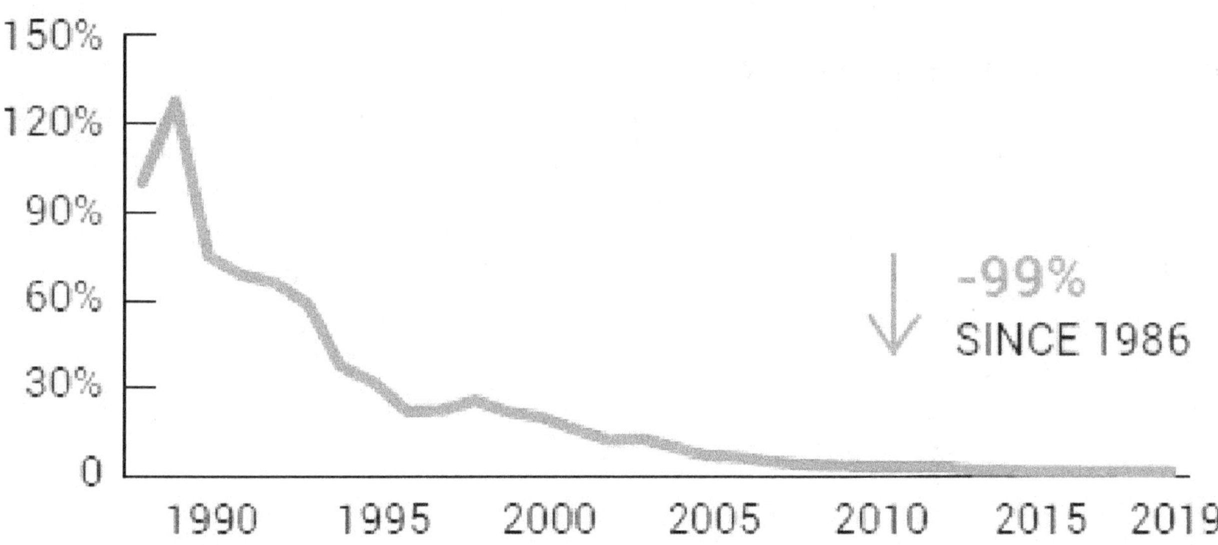

Source: UNEP, 2021.

Indian Perspectives

Post Stockholm, and Rio, nations across the world have adopted many laws pertaining to the three pillars of sustainable development-*economic, environmental,* and social. India too has implemented an abundance of laws in quick response to the rapid degradation of her natural environment. However, in the implementation of these laws India often falters. The Supreme Court of India has upheld in many instances that Indian laws are bound by international treaties and conventions of which India is a signatory.

The judiciary in India has often taken the lead in enforcing these laws, often calling into question the lackadaisical attitude of the government. Indian laws on Sustainable Development can broadly be seen to have developed in four distinct but overlapping phases. They are:

The emphasis in this phase was also on energy conservation and use of renewable sources of energy. Consequently, the *Energy Conservation Act, 2001* was enacted, which also set up the *Bureau of Energy Efficiency.*

The *Electricity Act of 2003* has tried to ensure better development in the power sector and emphasize the use of renewable energy.

Under the orders of the Supreme Court, *Compensatory Afforestation Management and Planning Agency (CAMPA),* was set up in 2004, to compensate for deforestation for development work through afforestation.

Environment protection is not a territorial but a global concern. Hence the efforts to protect the environment in India are indelibly linked to similar efforts across the world. The environmental policy of a country not only affects the environment of that country, but the entire regional ecosphere. The 'Kyoto Protocol' is the example of a sweeping measure undertaken at an international level (under the aegis of the United Nations) aimed at mitigating emission of Greenhouse gases (Carbon Dioxide, Methane, Nitrous Oxide, Sulphur Hexafluoride and two groups of gases hydro- fluorocarbons & perfluorocarbons) by industrialized countries.

What exactly is Climate Change?

The 'Kyoto Protocol' is a part of the *United Nations Framework Convention on Climate Change (UNFCC).* UNFCC sets an overall framework for inter-governmental efforts aimed at tackling the challenges of climate change. *'Climate Change'* refers to the fact that due to developmental human activities the original climate of the world is changing, and the average temperature is rising every year.

The increase in temperature is primarily because of the emission of

Greenhouse Gases, emitted mainly from industries. This also adds to the depletion of the Ozone layer which prevents the harmful effects of the sun (Ultraviolet Radiation) from reaching the Earth.

Why the Kyoto Protocol?

It is a movement to protect the world from becoming a world unsuitable for human existence. The 'Kyoto Protocol' sets binding obligations on industrialized countries to reduce emission of Greenhouse Gases.

The Protocol was adopted on December 11, 1997, in Kyoto, Japan and came into force on February 16, 2005. Over 190 countries are the members of the Protocol;

India & The United Nations

India is a member of the protocol. Significantly though the United States of America is not among the members of the Protocol.

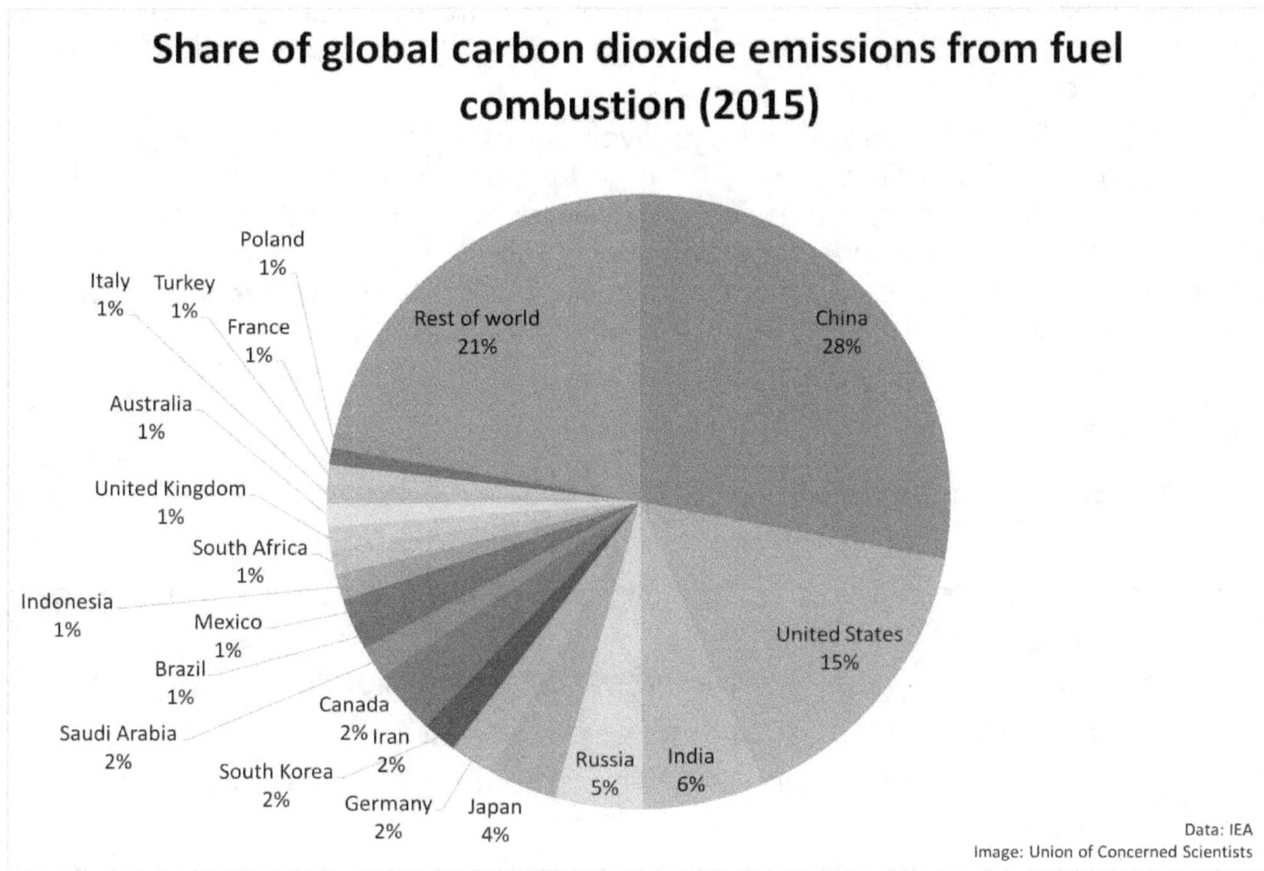

Some of the principal concepts of the 'Kyoto Protocol' are:

- Under the Protocol 37 industrialized countries and the European Union (made up of 15 European countries called Annexure 1 nations) have committed themselves to binding obligations to reduce emission of Greenhouse Gases.

- To meet the objectives of the Protocol, "Annexure I nations" are required to draft policies and measures for the reduction of Greenhouse Gases. In addition, they are required to increase the absorption of these gases.

- Accounting, reporting and review to ensure the implementation of the Protocol

- Setting up a **Compliance Committee** to enforce compliance with the commitments under the Protocol.

'Kyoto Protocol' is an important breakthrough as it is an acknowledgement of the fact that in the name of industrial development cannot be at the altar of the environment. Industrialized countries are bound by the salient commitments under the protocol to bequeath a safe environment to future generations that is habitable to humans, flora, and fauna.

Reducing the emission of the Greenhouse Gases has become a collective responsibility in making the global environment cleaner and healthier and thereby realizing the sustainable development goal. This obviously is an ongoing endeavor and not a one-time shot in the dark that hits bullseye. The success of the protocol depends on a show of global will to address a common menace.

International Instruments are a lot like domestic legislations. They are drafted by different countries coming together at the global level to make laws applicable to them. The Kyoto Protocol is not the only instrument directed at curbing environmental decline. In fact, there are several such measures that have been undertaken at the global level.

These international instruments collectively constitute what is known as the **International Environmental Law.** These laws have influenced the growth of environmental law in many countries to a great extent. India's main environmental legislation, the **Environment Protection Act, 1986** was enacted to facilitate the implementation of the resolutions taken at the **United Nations Conference on the Human Environment** held at Stockholm in June 1972.

Some of the important International Instruments are –

The Stockholm Declaration, 1972

- Laid the foundation of the modern global environmental law
- Recognizes different approaches required to tackle problems of developed and developing countries
- Recognizes that a healthy environment is an extension to the 'right to life'
- Introduces the concept of 'inter-generational equity'
- Calls for balancing the needs of environment with those of development (sustainability)
- Nations have the sovereign right to exploit their own resources, subject to the responsibility not to cause damage to the environment of other states.

The Vienna Convention for the Protection of the Ozone Layer, 1985

- It is a framework treaty within which member states share research and information, develop technologies for the protection of the Ozone layer

The Montreal Protocol on Substances that Deplete the Ozone Layer, 1987

- The protocol requires parties to reduce the consumption of Ozone Depleting Substances (ODS) to stipulated levels
- Developing countries given a grace period of 10 years to comply

The Report of the World Commission on Environment and Development ("The Brundtland Commission"), 1987

- Milestone in the development of international environmental jurisprudence and policy
- Established the doctrine of "Sustainable Development"

Rio Declaration on Environment & Development, 1992

Builds on the principles of sustainable development, inter-generational equity, and sovereign rights in the Stockholm Declaration; Expands the concept of sustainable development; Reaffirms, amongst others, the importance and centrality of:

- The Precautionary Principle,

India & The United Nations

- The Polluter Pays Principle, and
- Environmental Impact Assessment

U.N. Convention on Biological Diversity (1992)

Goals:

- The conservation of biological diversity
- The sustainable use of its components; and
- The fair and equitable sharing of the benefits from the use of genetic resources.

In 2000, a supplementary agreement - the ***Cartagena Protocol on Biosafety*** sought to protect biodiversity of states against risks from living, modified organisms created by biotechnology.

In April 2002, the parties to the convention committed themselves to achieving the target of "a significant reduction in the current rate of biodiversity loss at the global, regional and national level," by 2010.

Agenda 21, 1992 established a comprehensive roadmap of action to be taken at the global, national, and local levels, for the protection of the environment framed at the Rio Summit.

The United Nations Framework Convention on Climate Change (UNFCC), 1992

This sets the overall framework for inter-governmental efforts to tackle the challenge posed by climate change. Under the Convention, governments:

- Gather and share information on Greenhouse Gas emissions, national policies, and best practices
- Launch national strategies for addressing Greenhouse Gas emissions and adapting to expected impacts, including the provision of financial and technological support to developing countries
- Cooperate in preparing for adaptation to the impacts of climate change. (The convention was entered into force on March 21, 1994).

Such international instruments clearly imply that environment protection has become a matter of critical concern in the international community.

These instruments acknowledge that there cannot exist a single solution or a one-stop-shop for environmental protection. It is a perpetual process involving collaboration, cooperation, and unending participation of world communities.

Global Wildlife & Habitat Conservation

Convention on International Trade in Endangered Species of wild fauna and flora (CITES), 1973

The aim of CITES, 1973 is to control and prevent international commercial trade in ***endangered species*** or products derived from them. CITES does not seek to directly protect endangered species or curtail development practices that destroy their habitats. Rather, it seeks to mitigate the economic incentive in poaching endangered species and destroying their habitat by shutting off the international market for such wildlife products.

India became a signatory to the CITES in 1976. International trade in all wild flora and fauna and species covered under CITES is regulated jointly through the provisions of The **Wildlife (Protection) Act 1972, the Import/Export policy of Government of India** and the **Customs Act 1962.**

Montreal Protocol on Substances that deplete the Ozone Layer (to the Vienna Convention for the Protection of the Ozone Layer), 1987

The Montreal Protocol to the Vienna Convention on Substances that deplete the Ozone Layer, came into force in 1989. The protocol laid down milestones for reducing the consumption and production of a range of ozone depleting substances (ODS). In a major move the Protocol recognized that all nations should not be treated equally. The agreement acknowledges that certain countries have contributed to ozone depletion more than others.

It also recognizes that a nation's obligation to reduce current emissions should depend directly on its technological and fiscal ability to do so. Consequently, the agreement applies more stringent standards and accelerated phase-out timelines for countries that have contributed most to ozone depletion (like USA and China).

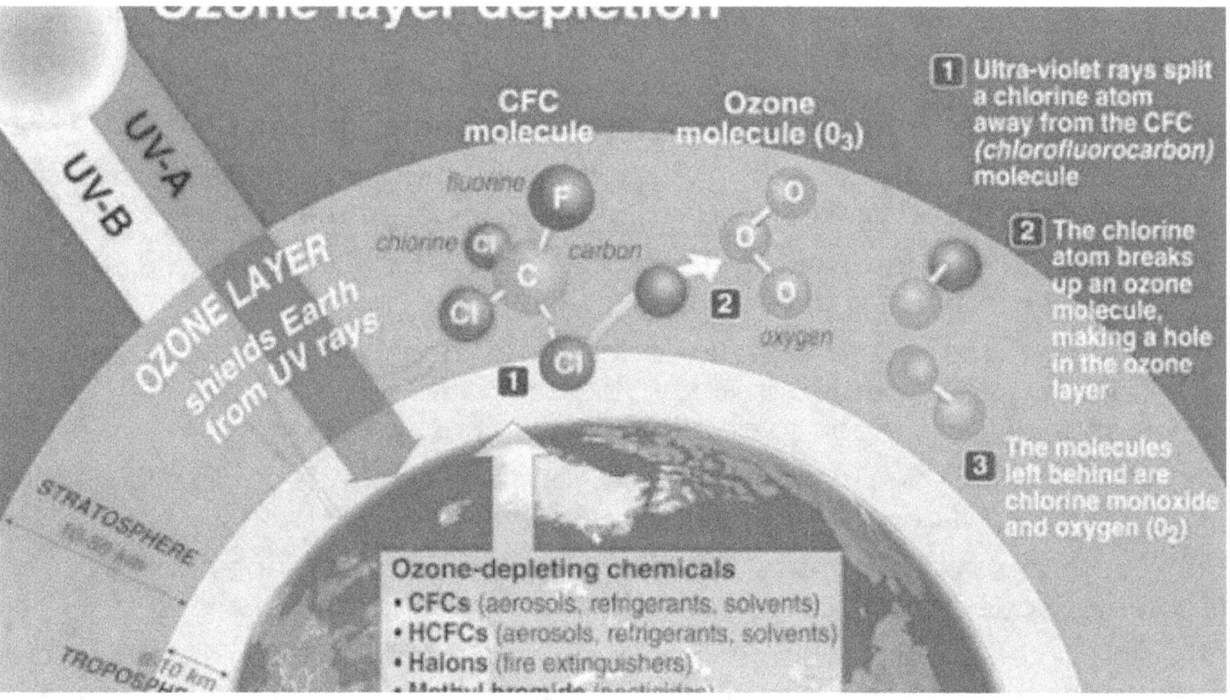

(Picture Courtesy: Public Health Issues website)

India acceded to the Montreal Protocol along with its London Amendment in September 1992. The MEFCC had established an Ozone Cell and a steering committee on the Montreal Protocol to facilitate implementation of the India Country Program, for phasing out ODS production by 2010.

To meet our commitment under the Montreal Protocol, the Indian government has also taken certain policy decisions:

- Goods required to implement ODS phase-out projects funded by the Multilateral Fund are fully exempt from duties. This benefit has been also extended to new investments with non-ODS technologies.

India & The United Nations

- Commercial banks are prohibited from financing or refinancing investments with ODS technologies.

The Gazette of India on July 19, 2000, notified rules for regulation of ODS phase-out called the Ozone Depleting Substances (Regulation and Control) Rules, 2000. They were notified under the Environment (Protection) Act, 1986. These rules were drafted by the Environment Ministry (MEFCC) in consultations with industries and related government departments.

Basel Convention on Transboundary Movement of Hazardous Wastes, 1989

Basel Convention, which came into force in 1992, has three key objectives:

- To reduce cross-boundary movements of hazardous waste

- To minimize the creation of such wastes

- To prohibit their shipment to countries lacking the ability to dispose hazardous wastes in an environmentally suitable manner.

India ratified the Basel Convention in 1992, shortly after it came into force. The Indian Hazardous Wastes Management Rules Act, 1989, imbibes some of the Basel provisions related to the notification of import and export of hazardous waste, illegal traffic, and liability.

More on UNFCCC, 1992, goals

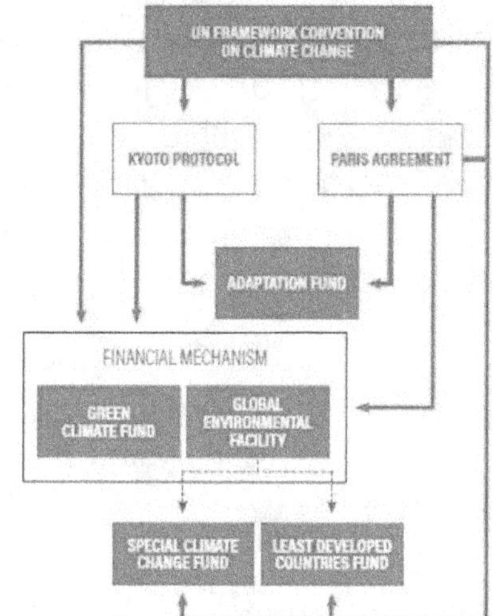

Note: The dotted arrows indicate that the LDCF and SCCF are administered by the GEF.

The primary goals of the UNFCCC were to stabilize Greenhouse Gas emissions at levels that would prevent dangerous anthropogenic interference with the global climate. The convention embraced the principle of not common, but differentiated responsibilities, which has guided the adoption of a regulatory structure.

India signed the agreement in June 1992, which was ratified in November 1993. As per the convention, the reduction/limitation requirements apply only to developed countries.

(Picture Courtesy: ResearchGate)

Only the reporting obligation for developing countries relates to the construction of a Greenhouse Gases (GHG) inventory. India has initiated the preparation of its **First National Communication** (base year 1994) that includes an inventory of GHG sources and sinks, potential vulnerability to climate change, adaptation measures and other steps being taken in the country to address climate change.

Convention on Biological Diversity, 1992

The **Convention on Biological Diversity (CBD)** is a legally binding, framework treaty that has been ratified by 180 countries. CBD has three principal thrust zones:

I. Biodiversity conservation

II. Sustainable use of biological resources

III.   Equitable sharing of benefits arising from their sustainable use

CBD came into force in 1993. Many biodiversity issues are addressed in the convention, including habitat preservation, intellectual property rights, biosafety, and indigenous peoples' rights.

Indian initiatives include the passing of the **Wildlife (Protection) Act** of 1972 (amended in 1991); and participation in several international conventions such as CITES.

UN Convention on Desertification, 1994

Delegates to the UN Conference on Environment and Development (UNCED), 1992, recommended the setting-up of an intergovernmental negotiating committee for enunciating a global convention against serious and permanent drought and desertification in countries across the world. The UN General Assembly (UNGA) constituted such a committee in 1992 which later helped the formulation of Convention on Desertification in 1994.

The convention is distinctive as it endorses and employs a 'bottom-up' approach to international environmental cooperation. Under the terms of the convention, activities related to the control and alleviation of desertification and its ill effects are to be closely linked to the needs and participation of local land-users and non-governmental organizations.

Seven countries in the South Asian region are signatories to the convention, which aims at tackling desertification through national, regional and sub-regional action programs. The Regional Action Program has six Thematic Program Networks (TPNs) for the Asian region, each headed by a country task manager. India hosts the network on agroforestry and soil conservation.

International Tropical Timber Agreement and The International Tropical Timber Organization (ITTO), 1983, 1994

ITTO, established following the International Tropical Timber Agreement (ITTA), 1983, came into force in 1985 and became operational in 1987. ITTO facilitates discussion, consultation and international cooperation on issues relating to the international trade and utilization of tropical timber and the sustainable management of its resource base. The successor agreement to the ITTA (1983) was negotiated in 1994 and came into force on January 1, 1997. The organization has 57 member countries. India ratified the ITTA in 1996.

Chapter 6

Indian economy and society since Independence

1947 and After

Indian Economy since Independence

India's strategy for industrial development could have been to rely on the pioneering efforts by business families that set up private enterprises prior to independence and the setting up of various public sector units run by quasi-government bodies.

However, the solemn pledge to make India a 'welfare state' was strong. The government narrowed its resources on investments in infrastructure, public health, and education; these being sectors not served well by the private entities.

Even though leaders were well-appraised of the growth dynamics of the private sector, and the established nature of India's vibrant entrepreneurial class, they sacrificed a 'private sector benevolent strategy' that involved a spearheading role for the private sector out of a commitment to establish a 'socialistic society' that they believed was 'morally superior'. Eventually, the country came around in the 1990s to adopting this previously 'pejorative' strategy.

TOP PSU LOSERS IN 2019

Company	Sector		Loss (%)
IFCI	Finance		−57.1
Indian Bank	Banks		−54.1
Central Bank	Banks		−53.7
MMTC	Trading		−51.9
Corporation Bank	Banks		−51.3
New India Assurance	Insurance		−46.6
Chennai Petroleum	Refineries		−46.6
Oriental Bank	Banks		−46.5
Andhra Bank	Banks		−45.4
Allahabad Bank	Banks		−43.7

Compiled by BS Research Bureau

(Picture Courtesy: Business Standard)

To assure the success of the government's chosen strategy in the 1950s, complementary measures were put in place. Most industries were given significant

India & The United Nations

trade protection so that their growth was not hampered by competition from more efficient foreign producers.

Industrial licensing and regulatory systems were established to ensure that private enterprises would not expand beyond limits that the national planners had set for them.

The system required all private firms beyond a certain small size to obtain a license whenever they wanted to expand capacity, produce new products, change their input mix, import inputs, or relocate plants. Hundreds of new norms enacted from time to time in the interest of 'PSU protectionism' stunted the growth of the private sector for the first four decades plus. However, with 'globalization' of the 1990s, the private sector overtook the PSUs with gusto.

The system that put the activities of the private sector under significant control of the government was almost immediately set free. Pundits and students of political economy who were not socialists derisively nicknamed this stifling system **"The License Raj,"** and **"Babudom"** that alluded to red-tape and rampant corruption.

Early outcomes

Industrialization was a moderate success in India early on. The newly created public enterprises, albeit after major cost overruns and several delays, turned out steel, chemicals, and other products that were generally associated with developed countries.

A British colonial official in the early twentieth century once derisively scoffed that he would be 'willing to eat all the steel that the Indians would produce'. If alive in 1960, he would have eaten 6,300 tons of steel!!

Still, by the late 1950s several challenges resulting from the planners' chosen strategy of socialistic (read as employment generating) economic development were taking shape, such problems intensified in the 1960s and the 1970s (especially during the war with Pakistan in 1971).

Many companies were run on political rather than economic considerations. As a result, they incurred heavy losses draining the government of its resources rather than (as the planners had intended) augmenting them. They were labour-intensive. Several enterprises were overstaffed and faced insufficient demand for what they produced, thereby forcing them to render idle some of their capacity.

A large number of nationalized banks and financial institutions owned and managed by the governments (as public sector undertakings) are still making huge losses resulting in the privatisation of the BFSI sector in India.

Human Development Index (HDI)

India trails many of her south Asian neighbours on the Human Development Index (HDI) primarily because of inequalities, according to a recent report by the United Nations Development Fund. These inequalities, hamper India's economic growth, it is stated.

India ranked 130 out of 189 countries on the HDI (2018) with a score of 0.640 which places it in the "medium" category of development.

She fared worse than Sri Lanka (HDI 0.77, rank 76) and China (0.75, 86) but better than Pakistan (0.56 and 150), Nepal (0.57, 149) and Bangladesh (0.68,136).

India lost 26.8 points on the HDI due to inequalities while the south Asian average for this factor is 26.1 points.

Since HDI is driven by health, education and income vectors, India should focus on improving on these parameters to show progress economically by reducing inequalities.

If India aims to triple its economy size to USD 5 trillion (Rs 350 lakh crore) by 2022 as Prime Minister Narendra Modi publicised in August 2018 and grow at 8 per cent per year as he predicted, it will require to invest more in healthcare and education. The global pandemic that entered India in early 2020 has also dislodged the economy further from this target.

Consider this: Despite being the sixth largest economy in the world, with a gross domestic product (GDP) of USD 2.59 trillion (Rs 180 lakh crore), India accounts for about 30.8 per cent of the world's stunted children. Not just short for their age, but one in five children in India are underweight. Undernourished children struggle to keep healthy and find it hard to catch up with their peers in classrooms and at workplace.

(Picture courtesy: Indiaspend)

India & The United Nations

Gender imbalance

There were 919 girls born for every 1,000 boys in the last five years–the numbers are worse for urban areas (899) than rural areas (925)–which shows a 'male preference', as indicated by the National Family Health Survey (NFHS-4) 2015-16.

When it comes to literacy, women fare poorly (68.4 per cent) with men (85.7 per cent). Only 35.7 per cent of the women have completed over 10 years of schooling, the survey revealed.

While boys and girls had almost the same enrolment rate in school till age 16, by the time they turned 18, remarkable differences show up. While both girls and boys struggled to do simple tasks like counting, telling time and adding weights, girls performed inferior, as per the 2017 Annual Status of Education Report.

(Picture Courtesy: Indian Express)

Widespread economic inequality

India is among the most 'unequal' countries in the world with the top 10 per cent controlling 55 per cent of the total wealth against 31 per cent in 1980, according to the 2018 World Inequality report. The bottom 50 percent control only 15.3 per cent of the total wealth. The report shows that while the wealth of the top one per cent has been increasing since 1980s, the wealth of the bottom 50 per cent has been declining.

Many castes and communities are more underprivileged than others. Muslims and Buddhists have the least share of assets and it has declined from 2002 to 2012, showed the 2018 Oxfam India report.

Scheduled tribes, despite accounting for 8 per cent of India's population, account for 45.9 per cent share in the lowest wealth group.

(Picture Courtesy: Getty Images)

Much of this wealth is less likely to be distributed anytime soon. Indians are least likely to break out of the income and educational bracket of their parents than the citizens of five other large developing countries–Brazil, China, Egypt, Indonesia and Nigeria– June 2018, citing a World Bank report).

The outcome of having lesser wealth is lower life expectancy, poorer health conditions and poor education. This appends to the fact that healthcare emergencies often push people into poverty. The figure stood at nearly 55 million Indians in 2011-12.

Post-Covid Economic Paralysis

According to the Indian Economy Survey (2020-2021) carried out by the Ministry of Finance, the pandemic has been a unique economic shock that has triggered both supply and demand side shocks simultaneously across economies around the world.

Increased uncertainty, lower confidence, loss of incomes, weaker growth prospects, fear of contagion, curtailment of spending options due to closure of all contact-sensitive activities, are the fallout of these shocks.

The triggering of precautionary savings, risk aversion among businesses and resultant fall in consumption and investment; all leading to the first order demand

India & The United Nations

shock. The supply chain disruptions caused by closure of economic activity and restricted movement of labour lead to the first order supply shocks.

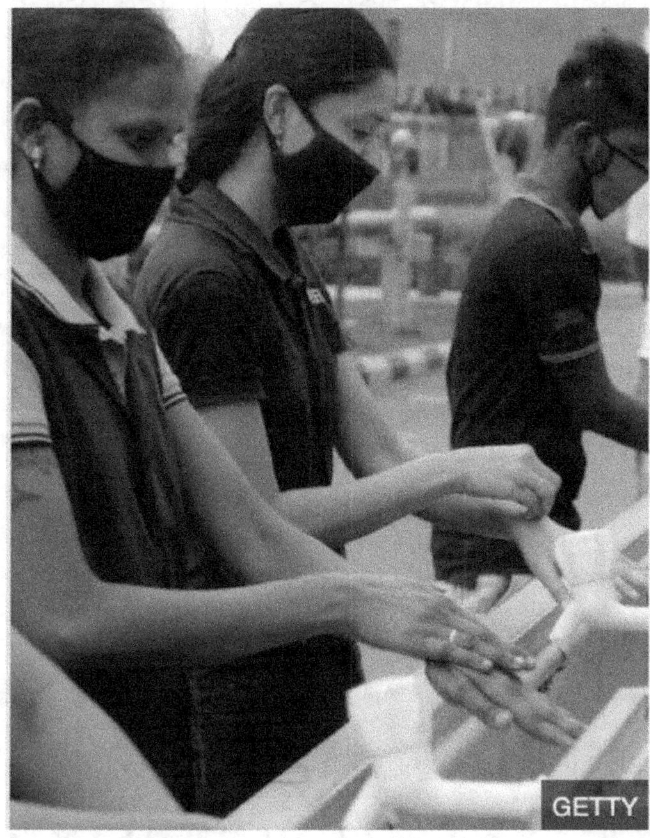

(Picture Courtesy: Gety Images)

GDP growth stunted

The National Statistical Office's latest Gross Domestic Product (GDP) data for 2020-21 fiscal embodies what was expected post-Covid. When the pandemic made its devastating entry in 2020, India's economy slipped into a deep crisis ultimately ending in a paralysed economy.

Lack of demand for goods and services in the wake of frequent lockdowns resulted in lowering consumption in rural areas that sustains two-thirds of the country's population. This, despite agriculture being the only sector that registered an increase of gross value (added Rs. 20.40 lakh crore in 2020-21). This year the normal monsoon facilitated this rise.

Between 2019-20 and 2020-21, India's GDP has reported a loss of Rs. 10.56 lakh crore, or a minus 7.3 percentage point growth. But the data on consumption reiterates what was mostly expected: the economic slowdown led to massive and all-encompassing reduction in private consumption. Without this, no economy will even sprout.

Private consumption expenditure that accounts for 56 per cent of the country's GDP in 2020-21 has reduced to Rs 75,60,985 crore (56 per cent of GDP) in 2020-21 from Rs 83,21,701 crore (57.1 per cent of GDP) in 2019-20. That is 70 per cent of the total GDP loss. This also demonstrates the criticality of private consumption to economic growth.

Debt Burden

However, the Indian Economic Survey for the current fiscal shows that due to robust capital inflows along with a weak dollar lent an appreciating bias to the Indian rupee since end June 2020.

RBI's prudent interventions in the foreign exchange market limited the appreciation. Combined with a rise in gold reserves and foreign currency assets, India's foreign exchange reserves climbed to a new high of USD 586.08 billion as on January 8, 2020, covering over 18 months of imports.

External debt as a ratio to GDP, which is comprised primarily of private sector's external debt, rose marginally to 21.6 per cent as at end-September 2020 from 20.6 per cent at end-March 2020. The ratio of foreign exchange reserves to total and short-term debt (original and residual) improved because of the sizable accretion in reserves. Reflecting lower current receipts, debt service ratio (principal repayment plus interest payment), however, increased to 9.7 per cent as at end September 2020 as compared to 6.5 per cent at end-March 2020.

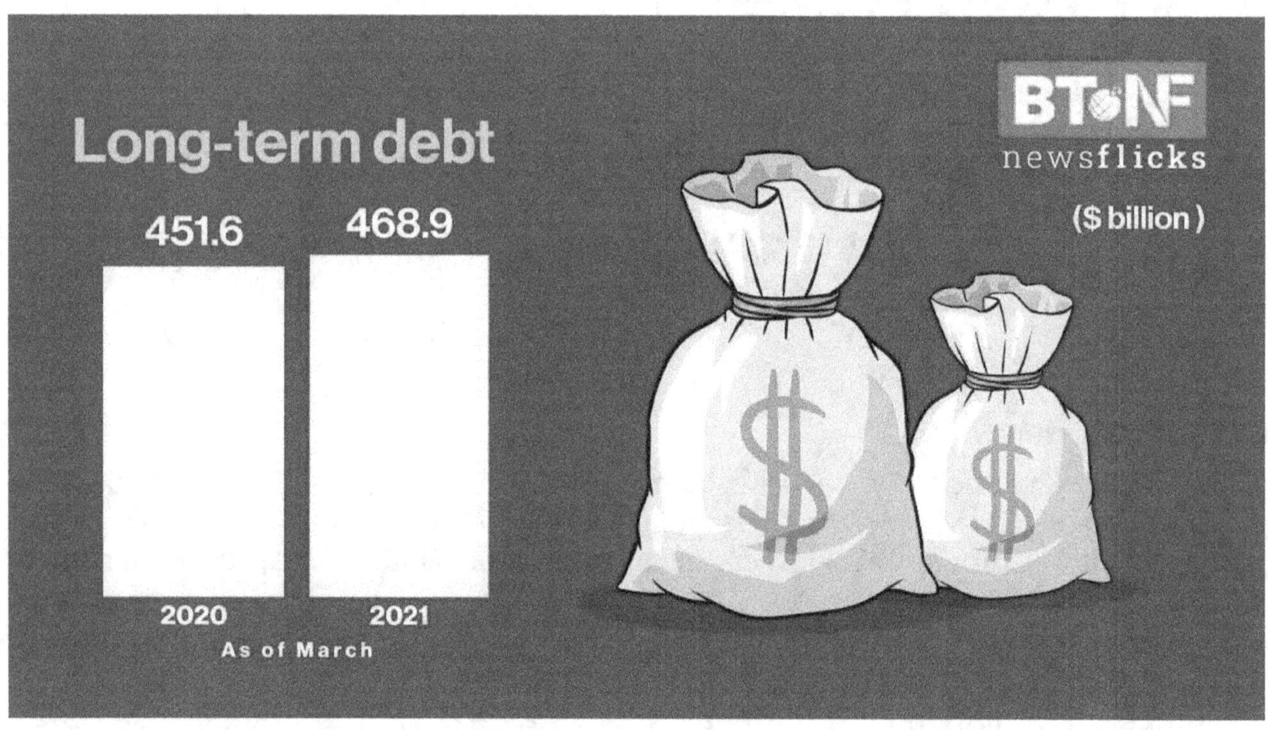

(Picture Courtesy: Business Today)

The Indian economy, after subdued growth in 2019, had begun to regain momentum January 2020 onwards, only to be stalled by the once-in-a-century black swan COVID-19 outbreak.

The economy witnessed a sharp contraction of 23.9 per cent in Q1: FY 2020-21 and 7.5 per cent in Q2: FY 2020-21 due to the stringent lockdown imposed during March-April, 2020.

Since then, several high-frequency indicators have demonstrated a V-shaped recovery. The fundamentals of the economy remain strong as gradual scaling back of lockdowns along with the astute support of Atmanirbhar Bharat Mission have placed the economy firmly on the path of revival.

India & The United Nations

There has been rapid recovery in India's economic activity from the COVID-19 pandemic induced unprecedented lows of the first quarter of FY 2020-21 on the back of extraordinary fiscal and monetary support provided by the Government and RBI. Overall movement of high frequency indicators over Q1, Q2 and Q3 indicated speedy pickup in Q2 and growing convergence to pre-pandemic levels in Q3.

As India's mobility and pandemic trends aligned and improved concomitantly, indicators like E-way bills, rail freight, GST collections and power consumption not only reached pre-pandemic levels but also surpassed previous year levels.

The year also saw the manufacturing sector's resilience, rural demand cushioning overall economic activity and structural consumption shifts in booming digital transactions. The full impact of the pandemic on the Indian economy is still unravelling and the future growth prospects would critically depend on sustenance of momentum of this recovery.

Agriculture is set to cushion the shock of the COVID-19 pandemic on the Indian economy in 2020-21 with a growth of 3.4 per cent in both Q1 and Q2. It is the only sector that has contributed positively to the overall Gross Value Added (GVA) in both Q1 and Q2 2020-21. This indicates that agricultural activities for rabi harvesting and kharif sowing were largely unaffected by the covid 19-induced lockdown.

Given the expectation of a bountiful kharif harvest, the food grain production target has been set at 301 million tonnes for the 2020-21 crop year, up by 1.5 per cent from the record output achieved in 2019-20. Sowing remained healthy while procurement continued unabated, firming up buffers and channelizing supply, while ensuring food security throughout the year.

In conclusion...

All the world's a stage
And all the men and women merely players;
They have their exits and their entrances;
And one man in his time plays many parts...

-Shakespeare

And leaves his mark, for the better or worse.

Never before in history has the world faced the scale of destruction it is currently witnessing. No man, no community and no country can escape the ecological disaster that awaits humankind if we do not change our ways. In addition, threat to international peace and security from increasing acts of terrorism challenge a meaningful survival of the humankind The Earth, for certain, can survive and thrive without us, the people. But what of us?

Without a co-ordinated and sustained global approach to contain the harm we have unleashed on the Earth, we cannot ensure a secure and equitable world.

The United Nations is continuously working towards achieving exactly that and India, as a member nation, continues to play a vital role. India actively contributes whether in peacekeeping or in building sustainable environmental practices.

THE UNITED NATIONS Preamble describes four areas as its pillars:

- Peace and Security
- Human Rights
- The Rule of Low
- Development

These four pillars are all interconnected and one cannot be achieved fully without achieving all of them.

Since its founding in 1945, the UN has been a witness and catalyst to an extraordinary transition in global relations. It grew out of the ruins of the Second World War and endured through the years clouded by nuclear threat during the Cold War and

democratic institutions and human rights violations which are often at the heart of national and international tensions.

131

to peace and security. In the panel's report to the Secretary-General six clusters The six clusters that threaten peace and security today are:

- Economic and social threats, including poverty, infectious diseases and environmental degradation
- Inter- State Conflict
- Internal Conflict,including civil war,genocide and other large-scale atrocities
- Nuclear, radiological, chemical and biological weapons

India's role in the United Nations is not familiar to many, even in India. It is important,

lives at political, economic, ecological, social and cultural levels. We live in a highly interconnected and interdependent world where our actions, whether at an individual level, societal level or as a nation, have the potential to exert a

The wide-ranging impact of the UN actions are beyond the scope of this book. As a concise reference point, the book attempts to cover, in brief, a few facets of UN operations in two areas: environment and peacekeeping. And attempts to explain the role India plays in the UN.

It by no means covers in entirety the role of the UN in the world and India's role therein.